About the Author

Malcolm Andrews is a respected 54-year-old Australian journalist. In his 34-year career, he has worked for major media organisations in Sydney, London and Munich.

For five years in the late 1980s, he was a daily columnist on the Sydney *Daily Telegraph*, before branching out as a freelance, concentrating on sport and profiles of newsworthy Australians.

Andrews has written 16 books. They include light-hearted looks at Australian life compiled in tandem with the late Bill Mitchell when he was cartoonist for the *Australian-Great Aussie Stuff-upps*, *Great Aussie Trivia*, *Great Aussie Sports Heroes* and their sequels.

Others include *Australia at the Olympics*, *Encyclopaedia of Australian Sports*, *Encyclopaedia of Australian Cricket*, *101 Australian Sporting Heroes* and *ABC of Rugby League*.

His latest two are *The Fabulous Fairstar*, a nostalgic history of the famous cruise liner which sailed into the sunset for the last time in 1997, and *Another Bloody Sports Book* (with fellow authors John Byrell and Frank Crook), a collection of outrageous sporting yarns.

Sporting Freaks and Flukes

Malcolm Andrews

ABC BOOKS

Published by ABC Books for the
AUSTRALIAN BROADCASTING CORPORATION
GPO Box 9994 Sydney NSW 2001

Copyright © text Malcolm Andrews 1998
Copyright © illustrations Pete Player 1998

First published November 1998

All rights reserved. No part of this publication
may be reproduced, stored in a retrieval system
or transmitted in any form or by any means,
electronic, mechanical, photocopying, recording
or otherwise, without the prior written permission
of the Australian Broadcasting Corporation.

National Library of Australia
Cataloguing-in-Publication entry
Andrews, Malcolm, 1944–.
  Sporting freaks and flukes.
  ISBN 0 7333 0698 5.

  1. Sports—Australia—Anecdotes. 2. Sports—Australia—
  Humor. 3. Sports stories. I. Australian Broadcasting
  Corporation. II. Title.

796.08

Designed by Midland Typesetters
Illustrated by Pete Player
Set in 10.5/12.5 pt Janson by
Midland Typesetters, Maryborough, Victoria
Printed and bound in Australia by
Australian Print Group, Maryborough, Victoria

5 4 3 2 1

Dedication
To the memory of Ken Andrews

I always thought you wanted me to be an engineer like you. It wasn't to be. Nevertheless, you inspired me to write ... to write about people famous and, more importantly, about ordinary, everyday folk. You're not with us any more, but I still love you so very much, Dad.

Contents

Prologue	1
Crawling Over and Under Water	3
Who's a Drongo Then	7
Johnny Won't Hit Today	9
Champion of the Colony	12
They Didn't Look the Part	16
Caught in the Indian Death Lock	22
He Didn't Worry the Scorers	28
A Drunken Genius	29
Grace and Favour	37
A Question of Adultery	40
Trick or Treat	44
Such Is Life	47
A Singularly Unusual Footballer	49
The Day the Poms Won the Aussie Rules	52
Bertie the Carpet Snake Bites the Dust	56
I'm Told You're a Footballer Mr Barassi!	57
Serving Up a Bit of Larry Dooley	59
French Farce at Flemington	66
Two Hat-Tricks... Yeah, Yeah	70
The Greatest Ego of All	71
Come in Spinner	77
'Gelignite' Jack's Perfect Drive	78
Not So Gay Gordon	84
Any Port in a Storm	86
The End of an Innings	90
Lou the Lip Never Lost His Zip	91

Going for the Doctor	94
The Million Dollar Mermaid	95
A Combo by Any Other Name	99
Further Back than Walla Walla	102
Double or Nothing	104
Give Me a Break	105
It Was Hardly Cricket	111
Last Ditch Effort	113
A Case of Mistaken Identity	116
The Judge Couldn't Split Them	117
Wocko Was Wide of the Mark	119
King of the Ring	120
The Ultimate Cricket Groupie	126
Big Frank—The Boxing Kangaroo	130
'The Flying Pieman'	132
Row, Row, Row Your Boat . . .	134
Like Father Like Son	139
The Record Flight of Mark the Magpie	140
Oldie but Goodie	144
All Arms and Legs	145
A Round or Two for a Pound or Two!	146
Newk Falling in Love Again	151
A Living Doll	154
The 'Modest' Professor Miller	158
Topping the Averages	163
D-Day for Normanby	166
The Greatest of Them All?	167
Into the Record Books	171
A Trip Down Memory Lane	173

Prologue

The history of sport has unearthed many freaks. Not quite all in the mediaeval sense of sideshow monstrosities. But while there were the boxing kangaroos and the like there were also the Australian sports men and women who turned their talents to vaudeville—swimming with legs tied or running along the bottom of a pool and beating the swimmers who ploughed through the water above.

Then there were those who by their natural talents could give freakish performances that you or I could only ponder in *our* wildest dreams. Performances which often forced the controlling bodies of their respective sports to change the laws in vain attempts to curb their prowess, to bring them back to the status of mere mortals.

The likes of billiards freak Walter Lindrum. Cricket's batting freak Don Bradman. So much has been written about him that we seem to know him as a brother. Bobby Pearce—such a freakish sculler that he was never beaten.

Then there were the sporting flukes that, by virtue of a stroke of luck or the mistakes of selectors, suddenly found themselves on the world stage, and usually unable to cope with a role that was far beyond *their* wildest dreams.

Sporting Freaks & Flukes is a book about heroes and would-be heroes. Of horses whose names have become part of the Australian language. Funny and poignant yarns about dinki-di characters. Celebrated nineteenth century strongman Professor William Miller. The bloke they called 'The Flying Pieman'. The cricketer who bowled only a handful of balls in his only Test, many of which landed on the adjacent pitch as wides. The jockey who rode the winner of the Melbourne Cup—and to this day no one knows his real name. Wrestler Chief Little Wolf, who wasn't a chief and almost certainly wasn't an Indian.

But who cares?

Back in 1954, I was hustled off to Sunday school at St Paul's Anglican Church in the Sydney suburb of Canterbury. My Sunday school teacher understood psychology. He knew the dozen or so 10-year-old boys had no real desire to be there. So he produced a most unusual bribe. If we listened attentively for 50 minutes and answered all the questions about Jesus, he would let us leaf through his wrestling scrapbook for the final 10 minutes of the lesson.

We learned about Jesus ... and we also learned about Chief Little Wolf, King Kong, Dirty Dick Raines, Lord James Blears and Gorgeous George. As they say, God works in mysterious ways!

Sporting Freaks & Flukes is for those who want to have a laugh, or maybe dream about swapping places with their heroes, or wonder what might have happened if they, too, had the fickle finger of fate pointed at them.

As with all my books there are a few people who I must thank.

It was John Byrell, my old partner in crime (from our shared ABC tome, *Another Bloody Sports Book*), who in his inimitable way took a couple of hours on the phone to get around to suggesting the idea for this book. My old Chief of Staff and now Sydney *Daily Telegraph* sports columnist Ray Kershler gave me untold help, as he has done over the past three decades. David Clark, trivia buff and mate, who let me steal a couple of items he'd turned up in his research. And I'll forgive Pete Player for being a Kiwi because I reckon he will eventually be recognised as one of this country's great cartoonists, if not the greatest.

It's not original but ... that's what friends are for.

Malcolm Andrews
Woolloomooloo,
New South Wales

Crawling Over and Under Water

Roviana Lagoon on New Georgia island in the Solomons is as close to Paradise as you could imagine. Azure blue water that sparkles in the tropical sunshine. Skirting the lagoon is the town of Munda. Well, it's not quite a town, more a ragged collection of eight tiny villages along a six-kilometre stretch of the lagoon foreshores.

At Lambeta, the Munda village adjacent to the airport, you can take a canoe and paddle the 70 metres across to Hobupeka, an island not much bigger than a couple of football fields. These days it is the idyllic setting for the Maqerea Resort. Just four bungalows, a restaurant-cum-bar and a dance floor. Tourists who lie in the sun at the resort are blissfully unaware of the historic significance of the island. Just over a century ago it was the birthplace of a fellow who was to change forever the way people all around the world swam.

His name was Alick Wickham. The son of Frank Wickham, a Scottish copra plantation owner and sea trader who settled in the Solomons in 1875, and a Melanesian woman from one of the Munda villages (no one is quite sure which one).

Alick and an older half-brother, Harry, would swim in the lagoon. Some of their mates would have long-handled, ceremonial axes tucked into their swimming trunks. Not just any old axes but ones their fathers had used to get 'trophies'.

For trophies read human heads!

For this was the heart of head-hunting country. The adult men, led by an infamous chief named Ingava, would board war canoes and travel long distances—even as far as Guadalcanal 300 kilometres away—and return with the heads of male tribesmen. They would also bring back women, still alive, as slaves.

In 1892, when Alick was just four years old, the British sent HMS *Royalist* to shell Ingava's island fortress about 8 kilometres from Hobupeka. It stopped most of the headhunters' excesses—but the grizzly practice still continued for some time.

As an old man, Alick would recall visiting the ceremonial canoe house that housed the ornate war canoes. Tiny heads, blackened by the smoke of the fires used to dry them and with their ears and eyes inlaid with mother of pearl, lined the walls. And he would tell of one raid in which the men returned with no fewer than 200 heads. They also brought back several men alive. They were later killed and eaten by the raiders.

One can only imagine the culture shock that six-year-old Alick experienced, when, in 1894, Frank Wickham took him in his schooner *Saucy Lass* to Sydney for schooling.

The Sydneysiders also faced a culture shock the first time they saw Alick swimming. Until then, all swimmers in the civilised world used to swim the demure sidestroke or the trudgen, a laborious stroke in which the legs instead of kicking would move with a walking action.

Alick shocked the locals by using a method that to them was revolutionary. But to a Solomon Islander it came naturally. It was the forerunner of the modern freestyle.

At one school swimming carnival at Bronte Baths, George

Farmer, a leading swimming coach of the time, was amazed. He turned to another coach and, shaking his head, confided: 'Look at that black boy crawling over the water.' And so the expression was born—Australian crawl.

One of those who swam against Alick Wickham was a more-than-useful Sydney sportsman named Charley Bell.

Bell was to explain about the newcomer's style: 'He used a single-beat kick with the left leg brought down with vigour as the right arm made the entry. The leg was brought out of the water up to about the knee then thrashed down with the shin and instep striking the water with force. The toes were pointed and slightly pigeon-toed.

'Alick Wickham's head was held fairly high, swinging quickly to the right and left, but breathing only on one side with each complete cycle of the stroke. His woolly hair had the appearance of not getting wet. His back was slightly concave and the stroke, a quick one, probably 50 strokes to 55 yards.'

Soon all Australia's top swimmers were copying the young islander and one of them, Dick 'Splash' Cavill, became the first person in the world to break a minute for 100 yards when he clocked 58 3/5 seconds in a 1902 race in England.

But Alick stunned Australians not just for his swimming style.

He was a true sporting freak.

One of his favourite stunts was to run 50 yards along the bottom of the pool and beat competitors who were swimming along the top. He had another favourite trick of diving down around 8 metres into Sydney Harbour with an empty four-gallon kerosene tin or regular ship's lifebuoy and sitting on it at the bottom of the harbour.

Wickham was also said to be able to dive into the ocean to a depth of around 30 metres and remain there for up to three minutes.

But his greatest effort must surely be that which he

performed one Saturday in the autumn of 1918. The famous entrepreneur John Wren had organised what he described as 'a patriotic carnival' at Deep Rock on the Yarra River near Melbourne to honour the Aussie boys fighting in the trenches of Europe.

Wickham headed the star-studded lineup of sporting stars. He was billed as 'Prince Wickyama'. He was unhappy about the name, but Wren smoothed Wickham's ruffled feathers with a cheque for 100 pounds—a king's ransom in those days.

To Wren, it was worth every penny.

Wickham was to dive from a height of just over 62.7 metres into the Yarra River. To put that in perspective—the drop from the roadway on the Sydney Harbour Bridge is only 53 metres above the water at high tide.

Wren's publicity machine worked overtime and on 23 March a crowd estimated at between 50,000 and 70,000 was on hand to watch Wickham. Many were certain he was risking his life. They became even more convinced when several times he walked to the edge of the specially constructed tower before retreating. Had he lost his nerve?

Hardly!

Finally he ran forward and leaped into space. There was a gasp from the crowd, as he seemed headed for the far bank and not the Yarra itself.

But Wickham had judged his dive perfectly. He hit the water almost at a 90 degree angle—and with hardly a splash. He disappeared for a few seconds into the murky waters, but then he broke the surface and a wide smile spread across his face.

The roar from the crowd could be heard miles away.

Wickham called for a blanket as his swimming trunks had been torn from his body on impact with the Yarra. A doctor came forward to examine Wickham—but he found no injuries.

With his incredible dive, Wickham had beaten the world record of 50.2 metres, set several years earlier by one GW

Clarke off a bridge in Chicago. Wickham's record still stands eight decades later.

Wickham returned to the family copra plantation of Hobupeka after the death of his father in 1935. The only other thing known about him is how he and brother Harry helped the Australian coast-watchers in World War II during the Japanese occupation of the Solomons. There were 4500 in Munda alone and luckily for the Wickhams their Australian sympathies and their assistance to the coast-watchers went unnoticed before the Japanese were finally driven out in August 1943 after several months of fierce fighting.

Relics of the battle remain in Roviana Lagoon—rusting ships, guns, tractors and petrol drums. But sadly there is no trace of the Wickham legacy.

Who's a Drongo Then

Drongo. Now, there's a word 'to cogitate on' as Rex (The Moose) Mossop was wont to say in his rugby league broadcasts of the 1980s. A good Aussie word. Almost onomatopoeic, don't you think? Drongo. Sounds like a real dill, doesn't it?

My old journalist mate Buzz Kennedy once gave the definitive description of a drongo. With due deference I repeat it here: 'A drongo is a simpleton, but a complicated one: he is a simpleton who might be expected to come the raw prawn; the sort who not only falls over his feet but does so at Government House; who asks his future mother-in-law to pass *the-magic-word* salt the first time the girl asks him home; who, when having nothing to do, sits in the corner counting his nose and getting the wrong answer. In an emergency he runs heroically in the wrong direction. If he were Superman he would get locked in the telephone box. He never wins. So he is a drongo.'

He never wins. And therein lies the origin of this word.

I happened to stumble across it while researching this book (although perhaps, in this context, I should hardly have used the word stumble).

The original Drongo, it transpires, was a racehorse who was galloping his heart out in the early 1920s. The owners named him after a species of black bird whose name was itself derived from a word used by the people of ancient Madagascar, the huge island in the Indian Ocean off the coast of Africa.

Now, Drongo, the racehorse, was actually no dud. But sadly, he just couldn't manage to win a race. Not once in 37 starts. Yet it has to be pointed out that he went close a few times. He was second in the 1922 Victoria Derby at Flemington and second again in the VRC St Leger the following year. Soon after that he was third in the AJC St Leger and a gallant fifth in the Sydney Cup. Gallant! It's one of the words racing writers use to describe what punters would call a dismal failure. If you've done your money, horses are never gallant in defeat.

It was after the Cup run—gallant though it may have been—that his exasperated owner decided to call it a day and retired the luckless Drongo.

His name soon became synonymous with consistently unlucky racehorses. Then gradually it changed to describe dud gallopers and eventually dud humans. A dill ... a drip ... a nong ... a goose ... a dummy ... a droob ... *a drongo*!

In the late 1970s racing authorities, tongue in cheek, scheduled a 'tribute' to the much-maligned racehorse with a Drongo Handicap. It was restricted to maiden gallopers and only apprentices were allowed to ride.

In retrospect, I suppose one could say that, at the very least, the winner that afternoon could no longer be called a drongo.

Johnny Won't Hit Today

Over the years Australians of European descent have claimed many Aboriginal words as part of their own language. It's one of the things that makes 'Strine' different from that which is spoken in the Old Dart.

Yakka is one of the words. It comes from *yago*, which in one of the Aboriginal dialects means work or labour. Then there's waddy, the term for a heavy stick. It is derived from *wadi*, meaning tree. And what about yabba (or yabber), meaning talk or chatter?

Stephen Harold Gascoigne was yabbering almost from the day he was born in the inner Sydney suburb of Redfern in 1878. His parents just couldn't shut him up. So it was little wonder that later, when he became a Rabbitoh in Balmain, his mates dubbed him Yabba.

Between shouting out 'Rabbitoh' to alert the locals that he was driving his cart through the streets of the working-class suburb with some of the tastiest little critters money could buy, he would chat incessantly with his customers. He'd argue about the relative merits of politicians like Edmund Barton (the cricket umpire who was to become Australia's first Prime Minister) and William Morris Hughes (coming through the ranks of the labour unions). And he'd talk about sportsmen such as swimmer Freddy Lane and cricket's Victor Trumper and debate whether or not a White Australia Policy should be implemented.

Yabba (aka Gascoigne) was to go on to become the most famous of all sporting fans in Australia. Barrack? You bet he

'Gawd give me stren'th and a walking stick'

did! From a vantage spot on the Sydney Cricket Ground 'Hill' he'd offer advice to all and sundry, whether they wanted it or not.

He'd first gone there as a kid in short pants. By the time JWHT Douglas brought his English cricket team to Australia in 1911, Yabba was already a familiar figure sitting below the scoreboard at the SCG, his cloth cap hiding a closely cropped scalp and a sweat rag around his neck, tied with a knot at the front.

By today's standards his repartee was pretty corny. But in his era his comments, shouted in a distinctive, gravelly voice, would regularly raise a laugh from both the crowd and sportsmen alike.

Douglas soon became a favourite target. He was a dour batsman who would stay around for hours while hardly hitting a run. So often he was excruciatingly boring. His full name was John William Henry Tyler Douglas. But such was the stuffiness of the English cricket establishment that he was only supposed to be referred to as Mr JWHT Douglas. These were the days of 'Gentlemen and Players'. It was made quite clear that JWHT was a gentleman.

Yabba soon changed all that. He reckoned the JWHT stood for 'Johnny Won't Hit Today'. And he was close to the mark. Much to the chagrin of Douglas it stuck.

Cartoonists back in the Old Dart latched upon it—and to the day Douglas died that's the way fans saw him. Whenever Douglas deigned to score a run, Yabba would inevitably roar 'Whoa! Stop him! He's bolted!'

It has been suggested that Yabba invented the cry 'Get a bag' for fieldsmen who dropped simple catches. Apocryphal perhaps. But, at the very least, he would shout to bowlers after loose deliveries 'You're length's lousy, but you bowl a good width.'

And for some reason he often roared 'Gawd, give me stren'th and a walking stick.'

Legend has it that in a Sydney Test in December 1932, when the Nawab of Pataudi got bogged down, scoreless for more than half an hour, albeit on his way to what was eventually a century, Yabba was less than impressed. He is said to have called to the famous umpire George Borthwick, whose normal job was that of a gas-meter reader: 'Put a penny in him, George. He's stopped ticking over.'

The *Oxford Companion to Australian Cricket* reports another rather risqué delivery (especially for Yabba's era) in which he alluded to a noted Sydney abortionist when bored by a batsman stagnating at the crease: 'Call Nurse Mitchell to get the bastard out.'

It *is* known that when the English cricketing legend Jack Hobbs played his last Test in Sydney, in 1929, the great man walked around the perimeter of the ground to accept the applause of the crowd. Hobbs stopped at the Hill, where the fans presented him with a souvenir boomerang. He waved to

Yabba, asking him to come down and join him for a chat. Needless to say the crowd on the Hill was ecstatic. Hobbs is reported as saying: 'He is a lot of fun. It is a pity there aren't a few like him at Lord's. We might not take ourselves so seriously if there were.'

But, of course, there never could be anyone like Yabba at Lord's. When he died at Lidcombe in Sydney's western suburbs in January 1942, the obituary writers understood this all too well. Said one: 'Just as there can only be one Victor Trumper and one Don Bradman, there can only be one Yabba.'

Champion of the Colony

When discussions turn to great Aussie Rules players the predictable names emerge: Barassi, Blight and Bunton, Cazaly, the Farmers and, yes, Captain Blood, Whitten and Ablett, Coventry and Jezza ... the list goes on and on.

But old-timers would always smile knowing smiles and dismiss them all. They'd heard the tales of footy's legend from their grandfathers. Indeed, some had been lucky enough to actually catch a glimpse of him around the turn of the century when they were still knee-high to a grasshopper. To them there was only one name worth mentioning: Albert Thurgood. Albert the Great!

Great? Well, he was certainly good enough to be three times the Champion of the Colony—the ultimate accolade in the years long before they even considered minting the first Brownlow Medal to present to Carji Greeves. Maybe, just maybe, Thurgood was the best of them all!

CHAMPION OF THE COLONY 13

And he always believed that his best years were spent across in Western Australia away from the hurly-burly of VFA and later VFL footy. So who knows?

He was a big lump of a lad standing just over six feet (183 centimetres) and weighing in around 13 stone (82 kilograms). Yet he was as agile as a ballet dancer and able to run even time over 100 yards.

The *Encyclopedia of League Footballers* quotes a description of the champion by historian CC Mullen: 'Thurgood had a lordly appearance on the field and looked like a military general at the head of his troops.' It sounded as if you'd want him there at Mafeking (before 'The Relief') or at Rorke's Drift!

When it came to taking a mark there was none that could compare with Thurgood. And what a boot! It is said that during his career four of his kicks measured in excess of 100 yards. The best was apparently booted at East Melbourne Cricket Ground in 1899 and covered 107 yards, 2 feet, 1 inch (98.48 metres). And who are we to doubt it?

Thurgood was a schoolboy prodigy who was offered a spot in senior VFA sides while still attending Brighton Grammar. He made his debut with Essendon in 1892, mainly playing ruck and centre half-forward, and kicked 56 goals in his first season—the first VFA player to top the half-century. He kicked 63 in each of the next two seasons, including 12 out of 14 in one game in the latter year. In both 1893 and 1894, Thurgood was named Champion of the Colony as the Dons set a record of three straight Premierships.

With the discovery of gold at Kalgoorlie in 1893, Western Australia was awash with money. And Thurgood astonished the Victorian football establishment by heading across the continent to grab his share. For three years he was the stand-out footballer in the west. He returned to Melbourne in 1898 but had to sit out a season because it was claimed he was not residentially qualified to play. Officialdom was quite pedantic in those days. Come to think of it, little has changed!

After the weaker competition in Western Australia and a year on the sidelines, Thurgood took a long time to regain superiority over his peers. But he did boot one of Essendon's five goals when the Dons went down by two points in the first finals play-off in 1900.

The following season he was back to his best, when Essendon became the first club in VFL history to score more than 1000 points in a season. In the semi-final he was particularly dominant, kicking five of Essendon's six goals (and providing the shepherd that enabled 'Skeeter' Larkin to boot the other) as his side got up to beat Fitzroy by one point. Some of the gloss was taken off the win by a Fitzroy claim that Thurgood's first goal hit the post and should have been deemed a behind. No one will ever know, but contemporary reports suggest the complaint just may have been right.

The grand final, against Collingwood, was no contest. Thurgood kicked three of Essendon's six goals as the Dons emerged triumphant 6.7 (43) to 2.4 (16). He was named Champion of the Colony for the third time.

A year later and the same two sides met again in the grand final. This time the 'Pies devised spoiling tactics to shut Thurgood out of the game. Throughout the game they had two men marking him at all times. He was unable to move, managing only one goal in the entire match—and Collingwood won its first Premiership with an easy 9.6 (60) to 3.9 (27) victory.

Thurgood retired after a dispute with the club, when it refused to give him a clearance to join the 'Pies, but he made a reappearance in 1906 when injuries left Essendon short of class players. The Dons reached the play-offs where the great career of Albert Thurgood finally came to an end. After kicking the first goal of the match, against Fitzroy, he broke down and limped off with an ankle so badly injured that he was never to play again.

Records of the period are incomplete but it is known that, all told, Thurgood played more than 200 senior games in Victoria and Western Australia and kicked more than 700 goals—a mammoth total in those days when 15 goals by a team was rare.

A champion of more than one colony!

They Didn't Look the Part

For the benefit of the younger generation of sporting fans used to equating success with physique it is important to introduce the names of rugby league's Brian Bevan and Puig-Aubert. With this pair there were no rippling muscles the like of which in their day was only ever seen in newspaper advertisements showing bullies kicking sand into the face of 8 stone weaklings.

Steroids were as far away as the chances of the teenagers meeting Marilyn Monroe, the Hollywood goddess they had fallen in love with at the Saturday arvo flicks at the local cinema.

Bevan looked emaciated. Puig-Aubert was rotund.

Freaks? In looks, most certainly. But more so in ability! They both had a freakish touch of genius that put them up among the greatest figures in sporting history.

Let's set the record straight from the start. The latter's name wasn't actually Puig-Aubert. We all knew him by that moniker. But it wasn't the one his mother and father gave him at his baptism at Andernach, in what is now Germany, in 1925.

He was baptised Robert Aubert Puig.

But, when as a teenager he signed for the AS Carcassonne club in south-eastern France (from where the family originally came), there were so many other better-known players with the surname Puig that a local newspaper editor printed his name back-to-front to avoid confusion. It stuck and, ironically, he became the most famous of them all. When he died at the age of 69, the great rugby league fullback was still signing his cheques Puig-Aubert.

We'll get to Bevan in a moment.

But first the legendary Frenchman.

There would be few critics who would not agree that he was France's greatest league player—but he was also probably the only international sportsman to regularly puff away on a cigarette while playing for his country.

Because of his chain-smoking his countrymen dubbed him 'Pipette' and he would regularly take time off to stroll across to the edge of the field to cadge a cigarette from adoring fans. Stories are told of a match played in a snowstorm in Wigan in 1947 when he kept catching the ball one-handed while holding a cigarette in the other.

Puig-Aubert's casual attitude to the game was part of his obvious charm. He took kicks for goal as if he were idly practising on some remote field. He would bang the ball down in a divot, and would never measure the steps before loping in to send it on its way.

Puig-Aubert would also regularly refuse to attempt tackles on opponents because he believed that was not the fullback's job. But he would berate teammates for their failure to have done the tackling in the first place.

Yet there is no doubting his immense ability as a player.

He figured prominently in the era of the great French Test sides of the early 1950s. His playing career stretched from 1944 to 1957, during which he turned out in a then-record 47 internationals (16 Tests and four World Cup matches against Britain, Australia and New Zealand, 26 European Championship games against Wales, England and Other Nationalities and a one-off international against the United States).

The height of his success was when he captained the French Test side on the 1951 tour of Australasia. It was then that he became a hero to Australians and not just those fans back home.

The early form of the tourists was so pathetic that the Australian authorities threatened to send them home. The warning paid off. Puig-Aubert and his side suddenly came alive prompting famous sporting journalist Tom Goodman to dub them 'The Unforgettables'. Nat King Cole's hit would have been highly appropriate.

They won the Test series against Australia with Puig-Aubert kicking 18 goals from 18 attempts, a record never since topped by any tourist.

The opposition halfback in that series was Keith Holman, a man who has played more Tests against the Frenchman than any other Australian.

'I've never seen his equal,' Holman said when Puig-Aubert died in 1994. 'A terrific player and a terrific gentleman. As a goalkicker he had no equal—and no one since can compare.

'One day at practice on the Sydney Cricket Ground I saw him do something I've never seen before or since. He placed the ball where the corner post usually stands and with a remarkable kick curved it around between the posts for a "goal". I've seen soccer players do it—but never a player kicking a rugby ball.'

Puig-Aubert's performances during 1951 earned him the Champion of Champions title awarded by the French sporting newspaper *L'Equipe*. It was the first time a footballer from any code had been so honoured. Puig-Aubert played in eight French Championship finals, winning five (in 1945, 1946, 1950 and 1952 with Carcassonne and in 1957 with XIII Catalan), and nine Cup finals, winning four (in 1946, 1947, 1951 and 1952 with Carcassonne).

Few footballers have looked less athletic than did Brian Bevan. He was thin and balding, and he would run on to the field with heavy strapping on his spindly legs.

Indeed, estimates suggest that it took an hour or so to get the bandages on properly so he could make his way out of the dressing room and on to the field. Who cares how long it took? For Bevan's looks were deceiving. Oh, so deceiving!

Football—any code of football—has never known a scoring machine like him. In 18 seasons in British rugby league, the expatriate Australian scored more tries than any other player in history. He notched a phenomenal 796 in club games and another 38 in representative and so-called friendly matches—some 300 more than his nearest rival, Welshman Billy Boston. Yes, a third more than the next best. And in the modern game no player comes remotely close to what Bevan achieved.

20 SPORTING FREAKS AND FLUKES

BRIAN BEVAN
Didn't look the part

The great Australian forward Harry Bath, who played hundreds of games with Bevan for the English club Warrington, said of the freakish winger: 'Brian never had any counterpart in Australia in my time. Maybe Dally Messenger had the same magical effect on crowds in the early days of Rugby League. But no player ever provided sustained thrills for so many fans over such a long period as Bevan did. He always gave me the impression he had radar built into the toes of his football boots and that this steered him around everyone between him and the tryline.'

Yet, surprisingly, no one in his home country ever recognised his greatness. He had made little impact on rugby league before he joined Warrington in 1945, from the Sydney club Eastern Suburbs.

What was it that made Warrington recognise the talent of the Australian sailor who had arrived in Britain on HMAS *Australia* during the war? Your answer is as good as the next. But the British soon realised he had tremendous acceleration and a prodigious sidestep. Reputedly this was perfected as a boy by sidestepping around fans as they left the Sydney Cricket Ground. Sure it was! Trust me—my brother's a doctor.

Bevan had a penchant for multiple try-scoring feats. Twice, in Britain, he went over for seven in one match. Yes, seven! Four times he scored six, seven times he notched five, and on 22 occasions he finished a match with four tries. And trebles were common as far as Bevan was concerned, with a career total of 69.

Perhaps this should be pointed out to today's journalists when they begin to wax lyrically about players who manage two or three hat-tricks. Or even to the players themselves, who far too often are legends in their own lunchtime.

Caught in the Indian Death Lock

Back in the 1950s when young boys would play sport in the street, they would imagine themselves to be the stars of that era. No different from boys who grew up at any other time. But if the War Babies and the Baby Boomers were playing tennis they were Lew Hoad or Ken Rosewall. Cricket, Keith Miller or Ray Lindwall. They ran like John Landy, boxed like Jimmy Carruthers and played footy like ... well, it depended where they were in Australia ... like Clive Churchill or Ted Whitten.

And when it came to wrestling ...

Yes, the kids wanted to be wrestlers back then. Wrestling was big. Real big! Tens of thousands of fans would pack the Old Barn (the Sydney Stadium at Rushcutters Bay) or the old West Melbourne Stadium. And tens of thousands more would listen to Reg Grundy call the bouts on the wireless. The exponents of the grunt and groan had a certain legitimacy about them in those days.

Well, when kids of the 1950s imagined themselves to be wrestlers there was only one fellow they wanted to emulate. Chief Little Wolf! He wasn't the nicest of fellows in the ring. Indeed, he was downright dirty. But the women and the kids loved him, especially in some of his memorable battles with the likes of Dirty Dick Raines, Gorgeous George, who used to spray perfume around the ring before his bouts, and Australia's own world champ, Fred Atkins.

CAUGHT IN THE INDIAN DEATH LOCK   23

CHIEF LITTLE WOLF

Big Chief Little Wolf was virtually unbeatable. Even when he was getting the mother of all hidings in the ring, the fans knew that at any moment he could pull off victory with the deft use of the Indian Death Lock, a grand-sounding hold from which there was allegedly no escape.

But the Chief wasn't really a chief at all. He was Italian and his real name was Ventura Tenario. His mates called him Benny.

Naturally, he would roar with indignation if anyone dared to question his claim to be a Navajo Indian.

'My father was half Spanish and half Indian,' he would bellow. 'And my mother was a full-blooded Navajo.' He would also claim he was made an honorary chief by several Indian tribes in recognition of his success as a wrestler. Of course he was!

Benny would talk about his birth on 11 November 1911, in a cabin on a Navajo reservation near Hoehne, a small town in Colorado. It was a bleak winter's morning and coyotes were wailing outside the hut as he made his first cry.

'Listen to our little wolf,' his father exclaimed. And the name stuck. At least that's the way the old wrestler used to explain it.

When he was about 13 years old, Tenario began training with an Indian boxer named Benny Bolt. Bolt wasn't much chop, but to the young Tenario he was a hero—so much so that he adopted his Christian name.

When Tenario was 15, a travelling boxing and wrestling show came to town. He accepted a challenge to take on one of the fighters and suffered the consequences—knocked out in the first round. But he asked for a job and the show, short-handed, put him on. He'd help put up the tent, sell the tickets in the booth out front and occasionally put on the gloves. He also learned to wrestle.

The travelling show went bust in 1929 leaving him stranded in Phoenix, Arizona, where he survived by doing odd jobs

CAUGHT IN THE INDIAN DEATH LOCK 25

THE STADIUM

TONIGHT AT 8

Chief Little Wolf

WRESTLES

Sammy STEIN

Over 8 3-Minute Rounds.

BOXING—8 RDS.
FRANK FARRINGTON
v.
STAN SMITH
ALSO OTHER BOUTS.

Prices: 6/, 4/ Ringside. Ladies Half Price; 3/ and 2/, Plus Tax.

BOOKING OFFICES: Hotel Australia; Mick Simmons, Haymarket; Alan Kippax, Martin Place; F. J. Palmer; Ltd., 390 George St., City Tattersall's; and STADIUM, 'Phone FM1363.

around a local gymnasium. One day a leading wrestler called Yakkie Joe was in town and during training worked out with Tenario. Yakkie was impressed and suggested the young man go to New York and talk to his manager.

It took nearly three weeks for Tenario to hitchhike almost right across the United States, but the journey proved worthwhile. It was late in the year when Benny Tenario made his professional wrestling debut, in New York. His opponent was Walter 'Sneeze' Achoc. Tenario beat him two falls to one, pocketed $500 as winnings and his career was off and running. After all, it *was* the Depression and $500 was a veritable fortune.

Realising the importance of being a showman, he soon changed his name to Little Wolf and then Chief Little Wolf.

He would enter the ring wearing a full Indian headdress with a Navajo blanket draped across his shoulders. Reporters were told that the blanket had been woven by 'the delicate fingers of my childhood sweetheart, the beautiful Running Water'. Once in the ring he would shuffle around in what he claimed was an Indian war dance. More grist for the mill!

These were the days when there were *legitimate* world champions in various weight divisions. He wrestled several, without managing to win a title—Jack Reynolds (welterweight), Gus Kallic (middleweight), Hugh Nicols (light-heavyweight) and Jim Londos (heavyweight).

The bout with Londos, the man they called 'The Golden Greek', was at Madison Square Garden in 1935. The referee called it a draw. A rematch was arranged, but Londos suddenly left for London, claiming a prior engangement. The New York Boxing and Wrestling Commission declared the title vacant and Chief Little Wolf went in against an Irish grappler called Danny Mahony at Yankee Stadium. Some 80,000 fans were on hand to watch a gruelling bout that ended up in a draw. A rematch drew 90,000, but this time Mahoney won by a fall.

The Chief made his first visit Down Under in 1937.

Promoter Ted Thye, himself a former world champion, tried to dissuade him from going to Australia. He reckoned that Aussies would not go to watch a Navajo Indian. He wanted to send another wrestler who was a Sioux. Luckily for Thye, the Chief talked him around.

Little Wolf's first bout was in Sydney against John Stulman and he immediately earned the ire of the fans with his dirty tactics. But they couldn't wait to get back the following week to see Chief Little Wolf scowl his way through another bout. He quickly became the biggest drawcard in the country.

He returned every year (except for four during World War II when he was serving in the US Army) before settling in Australia permanently in 1952. Between bouts in the major stadiums, he would appear in the sideshow alleys at country shows and rodeos.

Ever the showman, he had regular jousts with the famous wrestling referee Harold Norman. If Norman gave a decision that irked Little Wolf, the grappler would rip the referee's shirt from his back and toss it to the fans.

The story goes that Norman's wife got so angry with having to repair his shirts every week that she made one out of sailcloth, stitched with gut fishing line. When next Little Wolf tried to rip the shirt off Norman's body, he tore his fingers to pieces on the fishing line. And who are we to doubt the tale?

The Chief was still wrestling regularly when in November 1958, a week after his forty-seventh birthday, he was struck down by the first in a series of strokes. He blamed the strokes on his hard-drinking life. By 1961 Chief Little Wolf's health had so deteriorated that he had to enter the Mount Royal Hospital in Melbourne. He remained there a cripple for the next 19 years.

Then, in 1980, he went back to the United States in a wheelchair to live out his life in a veterans' hospital. Such was his fame that his departure from Australia was headline news. He was 73 when he eventually went to the great hempen ring in the sky, in November 1984. His legacy was a host of wonderful memories of a past era when every Aussie boy wanted to 'rassle' like Chief Little Wolf.

He Didn't Worry the Scorers

One has to feel more than a tad sorry for Dr Roy Park, the Victorian who has a special place in the sporting record books for having the most inauspicious Test cricket career of any Australian.

Now, it should be noted in his defence that the good doctor was a better than average sportsman. While studying medicine at the University of Melbourne, Park had represented Victoria in both cricket and Aussie Rules. He took over the cricket captaincy of his state in 1912 and two years later was chosen for the Australian tour of South Africa. But World War I intervened and the tour was cancelled. He missed a second tour, opting out of the AIF team to play a series against England in 1919, to return home after serving during the conflict in Europe.

He finally got his Test call-up during the 1920–21 season, against England at the Melbourne Cricket Ground. But, sadly, he was to play just one Test innings. It was anything but memorable. He was drafted into the Test side at the eleventh hour as a replacement for injured Charlie Macartney. It was on New Year's Eve that Dr Park strode to the wicket, batting number three, after a century opening partnership between Herbie Collins and Warren Bardsley.

The occasion proved too much for Park, who was dismissed without scoring, bowled after deflecting a delivery by paceman Harry Howell, off the first ball he received, onto his stumps.

Park's wife had been sitting in the stands waiting to see him bat, knitting a jumper to pass the time. Just as Howell ran in to bowl to Park, she dropped her ball of wool. She bent down to retrieve it and in that fateful moment she missed out on seeing her hubby's complete Test batting career. For such was the wealth of batting talent in Australia at the time that Park never got a second chance.

A Drunken Genius

It's hard to separate fact from fiction when it comes to telling the life story of pugilist Young Griffo, but there is no doubting he was one of the cleverest men in the ring in boxing history. And he was one of the sport's most infamous drunks. Late in his career there was never a fight at which he didn't turn up pie-eyed. The remarkable thing is that, despite being legless, he usually won his bouts.

The Boston *Police Gazette* of 24 September 1894, summed up his lifestyle in a nutshell: 'Young Griffo is not only dangerous to the man who faces him in the ring, but he is a positive menace to the morals of the profession and of the community. He sets at naught the traditions that men need to train. He drinks beer, champagne and whisky and seldom goes to bed. He gaily says as much, and observes, with a most reckless swagger, that he does not have to train in order to lick all creation.

'On September 17 he met a beautiful specimen of the natural pugilist named Loeber at Coney Island. Mr Griffo had no respect for Mr Loeber. He punished wine, stayed up all night, and in one round smashed Mr Loeber to a standstill in

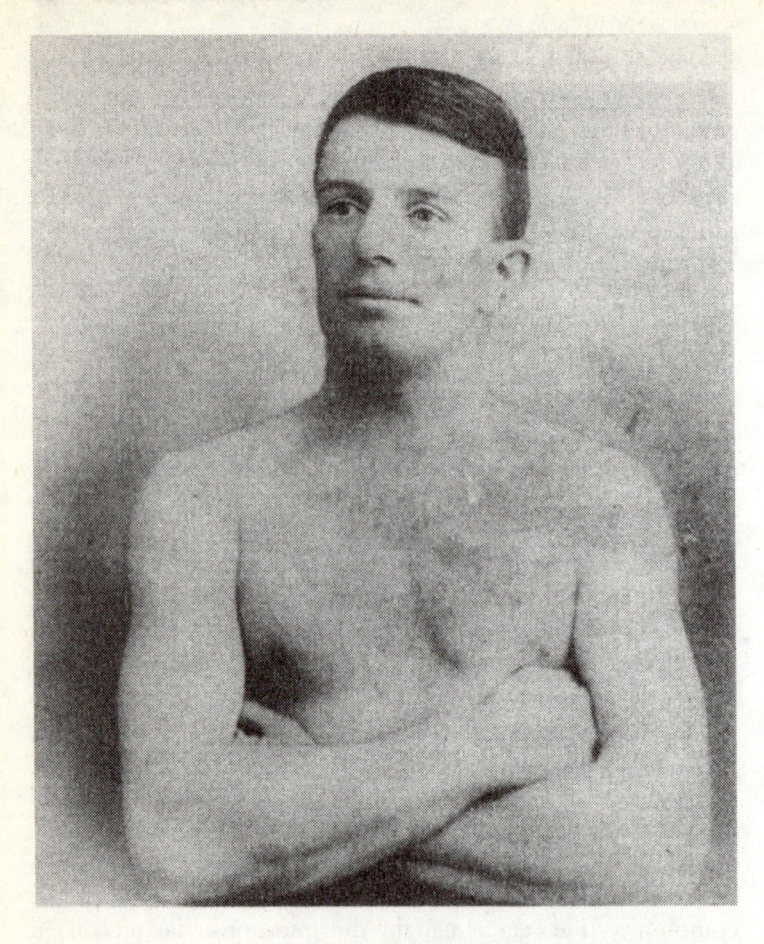

YOUNG GRIFFO

less than a minute. The lesson is a depressing one. There is nothing in it for the temperance lecturer to tie to, and the moralist simply has to ignore it and pass to other things.'

There is confusion about Young Griffo right back to the day he was born and the name with which he was baptised. The *Ring Record Book* claims he was born at Sofala, on the goldfields west of the Blue Mountains on 15 April 1869. The *Oxford Companion to Australian Sport* claims Sydney to be the birthplace. There are other reports that he came into this world at Bendigo, in Victoria. But the most accepted story is that he was born on a steamship en route to Australia on either 23 June or 23 July 1871. His father was Charles Griffiths, and when his mother died the young Griffiths was placed in the care of foster parents. They gave him the name Albert, the one he used until the day he died.

His teenage years were spent at Millers Point in The Rocks area near to where the southern pylons of the Sydney Harbour Bridge now stand. It was there that the poorly educated kid, who spoke with a broad cockney accent, came under the guidance of the great bare-knuckle fighter and trainer Larry Foley, who schooled the youngster at his famous Iron Pot Academy.

Not that it kept Griffo out of trouble. He was the acknowledged leader of The Rocks 'Push', the roughest, toughest gang of young men in Sydney. Such was their notoriety that at one stage the *Bulletin* noted: '... if Griffo has any real friends, they should induce him to emigrate, no matter where, as long as he gets rid of the rowdy element that now surrounds him'.

Author John Byrell, researching a book on sporting entrepreneurs Mark Foy and HD McIntosh, points out that Foy approached Griffo to sign up a few members of his 'Push' to help man the millionaire's 18-footers. The races on Sydney Harbour often led to fisticuffs—and Foy wanted a crew who could brawl with the best.

Byrell points out that Griffo himself never took up the offer to sail with Foy even though it was his cherished desire to do so. It transpired that Griffo got violently sea-sick on even the calmest of waters.

Young Griffo's first reported fight was a 1896 bare-knuckle contest against Joe Francis that he won in three rounds. The second reported bout, also bare-knuckle, was a win in 55 minutes over Tom Whalen in 1897.

But there are a host of other bouts prior to 1899, for which there are no details of dates or venues. They included four against a fighter called Young Joe Pluto and another against the splendidly named Kiama Pet.

Griffo fought 56 bouts before finally getting a shot at the Australian featherweight title. He was unbeaten at the time—even though many of the fights were declared draws or no decisions. These usually were when Griffo had undertaken to knock out his opponent in a specified number of rounds and failed to do so.

The bout for the Australian crown was over eight rounds on, fittingly, Boxing Day 1889, at Melbourne's Apollo Athletic Hall. His opponent was Nipper Peakes, also a pupil of Larry Foley, who went into the match at a disadvantage, having fought three times in the previous fortnight. It was fast and furious for five rounds and then the pair began to visibly tire. But they finished the final round with a flurry of punches before the referee awarded the bout to Griffo. The new champ offered Peakes a rematch but it never took place. The Peakes fight was Griffo's twenty-third of the year—no mean feat, even by the standards of those days.

The following year Young Griffo was to win the world featherweight title, although much of the rest of the world refused to accept his claims. The bout was staged on 2 September at the Sydney Amateur Gymnastic Club in the centre of the city. The 27-year-old New Zealander 'Torpedo' Billy Murphy had won the championship in the United States on 13 January 1890, knocking out the champion Ike Weir in the fourteenth round of their San Francisco fight. But when Murphy went home the Americans, without any justification, stripped him of the title, declaring it vacant. A Canadian, George Dixon, and an Englishman, Nunc Wallace, were allowed to fight for it in London on the condition that they then defended it in the United States. Dixon knocked out his opponent in 18 rounds eight weeks before Murphy made his first defence of the real title in Sydney.

As Griffo and Murphy were about to shape up, Murphy unsuccessfully demanded that the pair swap gloves. Foley, who was in Griffo's corner, then objected to the height at which Murphy wore his belt. There was a long argument before the pair finally agreed to shape up.

In the second round Murphy twice knocked Griffo to the canvas. Murphy had the better of the early rounds, but eventually the Australian began to get on top. In the fifteenth round Griffo laid Murphy out with a heavy punch. The New Zealander recovered but at the end of the round told referee Sid Bloomfield he'd had enough and quit. Murphy flung his gloves into the centre of the ring, still claiming they had been tampered with.

Griffo was ecstatic and did a dance in centre ring.

During the next 26 months he defended his world title four times in Sydney. His first defence, in March 1891, was against Queensland lightweight champion George Powell. He so pummelled Powell that eventually, in the twentieth round, the challenger had had enough, sat down in the middle of the ring and was disqualified. Griffo beat Murphy in a return bout, winning on a foul in the twenty-second round. He retained his title in a 25-round draw with Martin Denny and then beat Jerry Marshall over 12 rounds.

Griffo had one more fight before sailing for the United States on the *Alameda*, leaving Sydney on 15 May 1893. Over the next decade he was to beat some of the greatest fighters of the time.

He made his North American debut at the Tattersall's Club in Chicago on 13 November that year against a well-performed black lightweight named Young Scotty. An hour or so before the fight, Griffo was nowhere to be found. He had been on a bender for two weeks. The promoter eventually tracked him down and sent him into the ring blind drunk. Griffo stood there staring with glazed eyes at Scotty, who couldn't believe his luck ... until he tried to land a punch. Griffo stood as if riveted to the spot. He did not raise his gloves but just ducked and weaved as Scotty threw punch after punch. Not one landed. At the end of the round Griffo is reported to have shouted at sportswriters at ringside: 'Wait 'til I clear my bloody head, and I'll show you Yanks how to do it.' He did, beating Scotty in six rounds.

Griffo based himself in Chicago. He liked the bars and there were plenty of fights. He fought eight-round draws with Solly Smith, who a few months before had lost a 'title' bout with George Dixon, and a future world lightweight champion George 'Kid' Lavigne (this bout in New York). Then, in March 1894, Griffo came up against the former champ Ike Weir in San Francisco. A local police inspector intervened in the third round and ordered the referee to stop the fight because of the terrible beating Weir was being given. The referee did as ordered and then announced the decision as a draw.

On 29 June 1894, in Boston, Griffo finally got to meet the man who had laid claim to his title, George Dixon. Dixon had made seven successful defences of his 'crown' including one against another Australian, Abe Willis. It was again a one-sided contest, with Griffo, although half-drunk, outclassing Dixon. The official result was predictable, too. A 20-round draw. Griffo was to shape up to Dixon two more times—for draws over 25 rounds and 10 rounds.

Two months after the first encounter, Griffo was involved in one of the most outrageous decisions in the history of boxing—so infamous that the referee's name has gone into boxing jargon as a euphemism for cheating.

The bout was with one of the all-time greats of world boxing, Jack McAuliffe of Ireland. The Irishman had won the world lightweight championship seven years earlier and was never to be beaten during his career. At least, officially he never lost a fight. Griffo went into their bout at New York's Coney Island, also unbeaten, in 114 bouts.

To try to keep Griffo off the booze his manager Ed

Williams took away his clothes and locked him in a hotel room. He was surprised to hear a few hours before the fight that Griffo had been seen in a nearby saloon blind drunk.

Sure enough, when Williams went to the bar, there was Griffo. He had tied his bedsheets and blankets together to make a rope to get him from the first floor room to the footpath, then borrowed a bathing suit from a nearby bath-house. He was paying for his drinks by using a favourite trick of putting a handkerchief on the floor, standing on it and then betting patrons they couldn't land a blow on his head. They never did.

Williams took Griffo back to the hotel and this time tied him to a chair to prevent his escape.

Griffo sobered up enough to step into the ring where he proceeded to hammer the living daylights out of his opponent, who stood two inches (5 centimetres) taller and weighed 14 pounds (6.6 kilograms) more. But the referee, Maxie Moore, inexplicably gave the fight to McAuliffe on points. The *Police Gazette* headlined its fight report 'Night Young Griffo Was Robbed'. It was the last bout Moore ever refereed and doing a 'Maxie Moore' became part of boxing vocabulary.

The Australian was to make big money from boxing, regularly picking up from $1500 to $2000 a fight—a fortune in those days. But he drank the lot. Among his regular drinking partners was former world heavyweight contender John L Sullivan, who was as big a drunk as Griffo.

In March 1896, Griffo appeared in Jefferson Market Police Court in New York. In a drunken stupor he had been swearing at passers-by in Seventh Avenue. A police officer gave evidence that he had ordered Griffo to move along.

'Teddy Roosevelt couldn't make me,' Griffo had slurred at the constable. 'Are you a bigger man than Teddy?' The magistrate fined Griffo $3.

Later that year he was jailed for eight months for disturbing the peace. By this time he was deteriorating rapidly. In 1898 he spent several months in an asylum trying to cure his alcoholism. He retired several times, the second last time after being knocked out by Tommy White in the first round of a 1904 fight in Chicago. White, who had fought Dixon for the world featherweight title five years earlier, was well past his prime.

Seven years later Griffo came out of retirement for two last bouts, both six-round no decisions. The last was in Philadelphia against former world welterweight champion Honey Mellody, on 25 September 1911. In all, it is believed Griffo fought 170 times, winning 20 bouts by knockout, 45 on points and four on fouls. He was beaten only 12 times (seven by knockout) but most of these defeats came when he was on the skids.

Griffo lived out his life in a sparsely furnished basement room on 43rd Street in New York. During the day he would sit himself down on the doorstep of the nearby Republic Theater on 42nd Street regaling anyone who paused to listen with stories of his boxing days and the thrill of watching the 18-footers on Sydney Harbour. In the early 1920s friends raised money to pay for his fare back to Australia—but he knocked back the offer.

He died of a heart attack on 7 December 1927. Flamboyant Madison Square Garden fight promoter Tex Rickard paid $783 for his burial in New York's Woodlawn Cemetery. Otherwise Griffo would have been suffered the final ignominy of a pauper's funeral. Hardly the way for such a sporting freak to finish his life!

Grace and Favour

One can only wonder just who were the good gentlemen of the Parramatta Cricket Club who dared to challenge the Englishmen led by Dr WG Grace to a cricket match in December 1891.

Now Grace had a reputation as big as his beard. Bigger, in fact. And that's saying something. Indeed, he made it quite clear that he regarded himself as the best cricketer in the world—bar none. And the fact that he was 43 years old did not mean that his talents had in any way been diminished by the passage of time. Or so he said.

He scoffed when a fellow called Kirby—contemporary reports do not honour him with a Christian name—challenged his side to a cricket match as a warm-up to the first Test at the Sydney Cricket Ground. Grace is said to have refused the initial request because there were only 18 players in the Parramatta side compared with his 12—the finest in all of England. He demanded a minimum of 20 locals to 'make a match of it'.

Mr Kirby reluctantly agreed but only after Grace said he would not play unless there were 20. Grace had a big ego. You betcha. But he knew he was the one the crowd would come along to see.

Stories suggested that he lost the toss out at Parramatta Oval. But, as was his wont, Dr Grace refused to accept that loss and sent the Parramatta lads in to bat. They were all out for 67. Grace batted down the list for the Englishmen, determined to ensure the crowd did not disperse too early.

38 *SPORTING FREAKS AND FLUKES*

DR WG GRACE

After all, he *was* the drawcard and they wanted to see his expertise when wielding the willow.

It is not certain exactly what the score was when the good doctor strode to the wicket. Around 5 for 45? Or near enough.

A fellow called Wilson was bowling. Again, no one is quite sure of his Christian name. Grace faced three balls without scoring. Some suggested he refused to run, preferring to keep his scoring shots to boundaries. Wilson did not complain.

At the other end Johnny Briggs faced a maiden over. And it was back to Dr Grace once again. He fended off two balls. Then, with the third, Mr Wilson got through his guard and scattered the stumps.

Dr WG Grace bowled for a duck. He was livid. A fluke, perhaps? One will never know. It is just sad that history has never recorded just who this Parramatta bowler, Mr Wilson, really was. But no doubt he ended his life telling his grandchildren about the great day on 9 December 1891 when he bowled WG for a duck. On the other hand, Grace, back in England, never mentioned his meeting with Mr Wilson at Parramatta.

Mmmm. Strange that!

A Question of Adultery

To say that Arthur Coningham was eccentric is like saying Winnie the Pooh was partial to a feed of honey or that Phar Lap could gallop. The good Mr Coningham was eccentric to extremes.

Quaint, whimsical, odd, peculiar, outlandish, strange, erratic . . . he was all that and more. A Hollywood scriptwriter could not have come up with a more outrageous character.

Coningham holds a special place in cricket's record books for a ground-breaking Test bowling performance. But he was most definitely more memorable for his bizarre behaviour—both on and off the cricket field.

Yet Coningham was certainly no fool, no buffoon. He was well educated, having graduated from university with a degree in pharmacy. And there is no denying his all-round sporting ability. He was an accomplished pigeon shooter, footballer and rower, and contemporaries grudgingly acknowledged his prowess with the billiards cue. Such was this ability that it is said he financed his education by hustling at billiard rooms around South Melbourne during the late 1870s.

But cricket was his real forté. Coningham was a fine left-arm fast bowler and a more-than-useful left-handed batsman. He began playing club cricket in Melbourne before heading interstate to Brisbane where in 1890 he was part of club cricket history. Playing for Stanley against the Alberts he scored 26 runs off just seven balls. 'So what?' one may well ask. Well, the Stanley side was all out for 26. It is believed to be the only time in Brisbane grade cricket that the one player has scored all his team's runs. There weren't even any sundries.

In 1893, the first of many controversies involving Coningham occurred. The Australasian Cricket Council instructed the selectors to choose him in the side to tour England. The Australian cricket chiefs believed that by having a Queenslander in the side they could appease the MCC hierarchy, which was demanding that the team must represent the majority of the Australian colonies and not just the cricket strongholds of New South Wales, Victoria and South Australia.

Captain Jack Blackham and the rest of the team resented Coningham being in the side and were openly hostile. Needless to say he didn't get much of a go on tour, playing in only 16 of the 36 matches and missing out on all the Tests. And this despite returning a career best for a match of 9 wickets for 100 runs against Liverpool and District. He and fellow paceman Bob McLeod bowled unchanged through the two innings in that match, with McLeod taking 10 for 56. But Blackham refused to acknowledge that McLeod was always more effective with Coningham bowling at the other end.

The tourists made little impact. And a bitter Coningham blamed his teammates', heavy drinking for the dismal performances.

'When a man's full of champagne overnight, he's not fit for much the next day,' was the way he summed up the situation.

Coningham had been married on the day the team left for England. But that didn't seem to curb his appetite for flirting with the English lasses. Indeed, they found this Aussie show-off incredibly attractive and he had his loyal band of what today would be called 'groupies'.

And he took every opportunity to court favour with them with outrageous antics. When the Australians played the first match of their tour, against Lord Sheffield's XI, at Sheffield

Park, the legendary Dr WG Grace was dismissed for 63, caught by Hugh Trumble off Coningham's bowling. A delighted Coningham proceeded to walk the length of the pitch on his hands, furiously kicking both legs in the air. The austere English cricket officials were not amused—but the ladies in the crowd loved it.

The following year, in Australia, Coningham made an appearance in the Test arena. He was chosen to play in the second Test at the Melbourne Cricket Ground. He opened the Australian attack and immediately bowled himself into the record books. It was 29 December 1894 when, with his first ball, Coningham had Archie MacLaren caught in the slips by GHS 'Harry' Trott for a duck. It was the first time in history that any bowler had managed a wicket off the first ball in a Test.

His critics claimed the MacLaren dismissal was little more than a fluke. And Coningham's 2-17 and 0-59 as England won the Test by 94 runs was not enough to keep him in the side. It was to be his one and only Test appearance.

He had had a couple of stints in Sydney and in 1896 decided to move there permanently. But just before he left Brisbane he hit 151 and 51 for Queensland against New South Wales, becoming the first Queensland batsman to score a century in first-class cricket.

Down south he worked for a while as a tobacconist and a barber. But he became best known as a rails bookmaker fielding at Randwick Racecourse. The punters could hardly fail to miss him as he had emblazoned in huge letters across his bookmaker's bag and odds board 'Coningham—The Cricketer'.

But he really hit the headlines in 1900 when he sued his wife for divorce. Coningham was at his eccentric best ... or worst ... whichever way you want to look at it. As a result, the public gallery of the court was packed every morning with inquisitive Sydneysiders wondering what outrageous behaviour would be the fare for the day.

Such was Coningham's unpredictable behaviour that his solicitor walked out on him and the former Test cricketer was left to conduct his own case.

Coningham was a Protestant—and he rocked Sydney society when he named a Catholic priest and administrator of St Mary's Cathedral, Father O'Haran, as his wife's lover. It was an incredibly flamboyant display that played upon the considerable sectarian distrust among the people of Sydney.

But there was more. Coningham would regularly quote famous poets such as Keats, Shelley and Burns in an effort to prove his case. And one morning he caused a furore by appearing in court with a loaded revolver strapped to his waist. The appalled judge ordered him to remove it immediately—which Coningham did with a theatrical flourish.

It was all to no avail. He lost the case and was forced to remain married.

What is it they say? A man who acts as his own lawyer has a fool for a client!

Nevertheless Coningham got a separation of sorts by heading off to New Zealand. Not much is known about his time there except that at one stage he was jailed for fraud.

Coningham eventually got the divorce he had wanted... in 1912. But he was already a sad figure tormented by visions and the realisation that the eccentricities that were accepted by the fairer sex when he was a handsome young man were not tolerated in middle age.

Eventually he was admitted to Gladesville Mental Asylum in Sydney where he remained until, in 1939, death came as a blessed relief. He was 75 years old.

Trick or Treat

We're not sure if the following story is 100 per cent correct, but it deserves to be written down for sporting historians of the future to consider.

It concerns the latter life of Australian-born golfing professional Joe Kirkwood. He was in his seventies when he got the job of teaching vacationers at a plush resort in the US state of Vermont. The first thing he did was put a sign on the door of the pro shop: 'Learn the fundamentals of golf—swinging, swearing and cheating.'

This summed up Kirkwood's approach to golf. He never took himself seriously. It was an attitude that made him not only one of the finest golfers in the world, but a sporting genius whose exhibitions of freak shots drew huge galleries at every course he visited. And he visited a lot. It is said that he played on more golf courses that any other person in history ... possibly as many as 8000. Like the story about the sign, no one will ever be able to verify the exact number. But there is no golfer willing to dispute it. Like Lucky Starr, the rock 'n' roll star of the 1950s, Joe Kirkwood could boast: 'I've been everywhere, man!'

Kirkwood ran away from his Sydney home soon after the turn of the century, at the age of 12, and ended up in Cooma when it was just a sleepy hamlet and not the thriving town it became as the headquarters of the giant Snowy Mountains Scheme. Claiming he was 14, Kirkwood got a job on a local sheep station owned by grazier JRD Sellar.

Sellar was a keen golfer and had his own three-hole

practice range on the property. It was here that Kirkwood was to set the foundations for his later unusual golfing career. He got fed up playing the same three holes over and over again, so devised trick shots to amuse himself. And he soon became adept at hitting the balls both left and right handed.

Within months the 14-year-old had won the Cooma Golf Club Championship. Soon after this first success, Sellar took Kirkwood with him on a business trip to Sydney and arranged for him to be apprenticed to the golf pro at Manly. It wasn't to be too many years before he took over his mentor's job.

And Kirkwood soon began to make a real name for himself. He won the 1920 Australian Open in at The Australian course in Sydney with a four-round score of 290—knocking 12 strokes off the previous best set by the Hon Ivo Whitton in 1913. The same year Kirkwood won the New Zealand Open and the Australian PGA, before he headed off to England. There he finished sixth in the British Open. But there was not enough money on which to survive in Britain so he journeyed across the Atlantic to the United States.

It was to be his 'home' for the rest of his life.

He won the 1922 Canadian Open and the following year took out the Opens of Texas, Florida, California and Georgia. But there was still not too much money. It was then that his Cooma training came to the fore.

While Kirkwood was travelling from Florida to a tournament at Pinehurst in North Carolina a thief stole his wallet, containing his last $500. Needing an urgent cash injection he went to the practice green at the local club and started displaying a few of his trick shots.

There were a few that were to feature in his exhibitions until the day he died.

He would tee up two balls and hit them simultaneously with a seven iron. They would cross in mid-flight, Kirkwood having put a slice on one and a hook on the other. How did he do it? When asked he would just smile a knowing smile.

Then he would balance three balls on top of each other. He'd hit the middle one some 200 metres down the fairway. The other two would stay at his feet.

Or he would drive the ball with a full-blooded wood shot. It would not head down the fairway. Instead it would shoot vertically off the tee and land in Kirkwood's outstretched hand as it returned to earth.

On that first morning at Pinehurst, the locals were entranced and passed around the hat. There was more than $500 in it when it was handed to Kirkwood.

From then on, Kirkwood would precede each tournament appearance with his own special exhibition, charging spectators $2 each to witness his phenomenal feats. He never left without at least $500 in the kitty.

He had his own special bag of 60 different clubs ranging in size from a foot and a half (46 centimetres) to 10 feet (3.4 metres). Some were made of flexible rubber. Others had extra lead-weights in the head.

On one occasion he hit a hole-in-one using for his tee the face of a watch sitting on the forehead of a spectator lying on the ground—the fellow getting a closer look at the action than he had originally bargained for.

Kirkwood returned home to Australia just three times, in 1930 and 1937, with the great Walter Hagen (Hagen tutoring would-be golfing champs and Kirkwood showing off his freakish tricks), and in 1954. But like singer Peter Allen, he still called Australia home.

'Just look at my passport,' Kirkwood would say.

He quit the exhibition tours in 1965. Five years later, aged 73, he passed away. He didn't achieve his aim of dying during a round of golf. But until his last day, he was still giving lessons and amusing the Americans with his trick shots.

Such Is Life

Now, far be it for me to destroy an Aussie legend. But can anyone really prove to me that Ned Kelly ever truly engaged in fisticuffs in a boxing ring?

The stories have it that Ned was as much a freak with his fists as he was with the guns he toted when robbing folk around Victoria. I'm not an expert on robbery, so I'll just have to accept the wild stories we were told at primary school. But this is a sporting book and we want our sporting facts to be right. Did Ned shape up or didn't he?

There is, of course, *the* picture! A photo published in magazines every few years and said to be that of the people's hero in a boxing pose. No one is quite certain whether or not it was actually Ned himself or some poor old battler who just happened to bear a vague resemblance to the bushranger. I wished I owned the photo. I reckon I could have made more than Ned did himself from his wayward ways (allowing, of course, for inflation, the imposition of a GST, the need for magazine proprietors to make money for their shareholders, changes in taxes etc etc).

Then there is the story of Aussie bare-knuckle champ Larry Foley who took on a loud-mouthed English fighter called Abe Hicken in 1879—just across the Murray River from the Victorian town of Echuca. The venue was chosen because of friendly constabulary on the NSW side of the river. Contemporary reports suggest—and one has to realise that in those days there was no media to confirm or deny said reports—that after 70 minutes of torrid battle Hicken's

48 **SPORTING FREAKS AND FLUKES**

face was a bloodied, jellied pulp. His seconds were smart enough to throw in the towel.

A bearded man then pushed his way through the throng to shake Foley's hand.

'Today you made us all Irish Catholics proud,' he told Foley before making a surprisingly quick exit. Hollywood movie producers would have loved it.

'Who was he?' Foley is said to have asked.

'Ned Kelly,' came the reply. And Foley nodded. After all, Ned Kelly was a great boxer. A real freak.

One can only wonder. I consulted noted Australian boxing historian John Hogg, who has records of virtually every bout ever contested in Australia. Just how good was Ned Kelly's boxing record?

Sadly, it has to be reported ... there is no record of Ned ever fighting. Except, of course, against the police at Glenrowan in 1880.

Such is life!

A Singularly Unusual Footballer

There were some pretty strange occurrences on the sporting field in the so-called good old days.

Let's look back to 1907 when the New Zealand rugby union side was touring Australia. In one match in Brisbane they were playing Queensland, when one of the bananabenders was injured. Injured badly! They carried the poor bloke off on a stretcher.

These were the good old days when they allowed blokes to be replaced if badly injured. Later on they became more blasé about injuries. A man's game demanded that players be real men. Even if they had broken arms or collarbones ... even occasionally a broken ankle. Stoically they would play on. This was what legends were made of.

But in 1907 they allowed replacements.

The Queenslander came off. But the reserves weren't kitted out ready for such a situation.

Never mind. John Arthur Fihelly, Jack to his mates, quickly ran on as a replacement, in his civvies. Long grey trousers, perfectly creased. White business shirt. He took off his tie. And, in deference to the occasion, he did quickly lace on a pair of footy boots.

It was only for about 10 minutes. Then came oranges. And the Queensland lads formed a circle around Jack Fihelly as he discarded his street clothes and donned jersey and shorts. Now he looked the part.

The Irish-born forward played rugby union for Australia that year. But to this day it is suspected that he earned his spot in the fifteen—together with six other Queenslanders—because the Rah-Rah authorities in Sydney didn't want to be landed with the expense of sending more New South Welshmen than necessary to Brisbane for the tussles with the Kiwis. It should be noted that the Queenslanders had been beaten 23–3 and 17–11 before the selectors sat down to choose the Test sides.

Fihelly's unusual career did not end there. He was among the first to switch to rugby league when the breakaway code was formed in 1908. It was clever thinking. He virtually ran what was then the equivalent of the Queensland Rugby League. And he showed a firm grasp of the machinations that were later to make him a successful politician.

He holds a unique place in Australian rugby league history, being the only player to complete a Kangaroo tour without playing a match. And thereby lies another story.

There was criticism of his selection in the 1908–09 Kangaroo side—largely because he was one of the five selectors and, according to *The Referee* newspaper, he was too light for international football.

He wasn't alone. Of the five selectors, four chose themselves. And the other one would have undoubtedly followed suit, except he couldn't get time off from his business for the long tour of Britain.

Fihelly was also named as Assistant Manager and that was the easy way out. Despite there being 45 games on tour, never once did he take the field. Too much work checking out the finances was his excuse.

He is also remembered as the man who got an Aborigine to write the war-cry used by the Pioneers and several subsequent Kangaroo squads, even though Fihelly knew virtually nothing about Aboriginal culture.

By the way, Fihelly did eventually make it into the rugby league Test arena. Two years after the Kangaroo tour, he refereed the match between the touring Great Britain side and Combined New South Wales/Queensland, a game that today is recognised as the second Test of the 1910 series.

And in politics he became Minister for Railways in the Queensland government of the rabid right-winger EG 'Ted' Theodore. If nothing else, that must say something about Fihelly.

The Day the Poms Won the Aussie Rules

You'd win a wager or three with this yarn if you wanted to. It's a story about a team of Pommies that beat Port Adelaide in a game of Aussie Rules.

It sounds bizarre. But if you wanted to really clean up, try betting on the fact that the Poms were in fact rugby union footballers and cricketers who had never played the Australian game until a month before their fluke victory.

It happened in July 1888. And the seeds for this remarkable sporting first were sown in October the previous year when a cricket team signed up by three English sporting entrepreneurs, James Lillywhite Jnr, Alfred Shaw and Arthur Shrewsbury, arrived in Adelaide on the ocean liner *Iberia*. The English side was captained by C Aubrey Smith, later to become a famous Hollywood actor.

The three promoters were quite eccentric—although probably no more than any other Englishmen of the period. Lillywhite was England's captain in the first ever Test, between Australia and England in 1877. Shaw could boast having played cricket on a frozen fjord at Spitzenberg at midnight. And Shrewsbury was hirsutely challenged, but no one ever saw the top of his bald pate. He always wore a cap on the field, a bowler hat in public and a nightcap in bed. Or so the historians claim.

The cricket tour was an absolute financial disaster—even though the Englishmen, bolstered by players from another

THE DAY THE POMS WON THE AUSSIE RULES 53

visiting English side, won the only Test of the tour, beating Australia by 126 runs at the Sydney Cricket Ground. The match was memorable not for the reason that Shrewsbury was the highest scorer with 44, coping with the guiles of Aussie fast bowler CB 'Terror' Turner who took 5 for 44 (and 7 for 43 in the second innings) on a rain-affected wicket. No, it was the fact that Australia was out in its first dig for a mere 42 runs, a score that remains to this day as the Aussies' second lowest in the history.

Indeed, the cricket tour lost the three organisers some £2400, a king's ransom in those days. But Shrewsbury was impressed by the local enthusiasm for Australian Rules football. He sent all but five of the cricketers home to England and arranged for Shaw, back in London, to sign up 16 rugby union players from the north of England. They included four internationals.

Shrewsbury was convinced the Australian football code was primitive and his players would easily adapt. But to try to cover finances he arranged rugby matches in New South Wales and Queensland. The tourists won 14 of these 16 games.

It wasn't so easy when they swapped codes. The first match was against Carlton at the Melbourne Cricket Ground on 16 June 1888. Interest was high and some 29,355 fans turned up to see the locals thrash the Englishmen 14.17 (101) to 2.7 (19). It didn't augur well for the rest of the tour of the southern states.

They arrived in Adelaide at the beginning of July. And the local reporters were impressed by their physique if not their record in Victoria.

'They are mostly above the average height, well proportioned, active fellows,' wrote a football reporter from the Adelaide *Observer*. 'They are all heavy. Not one weighs under 11 stone, while two are near 15 stone and the average is 12 stone. In point of physique they far outshine any team that either of the colonies puts into the football arena.'

Then came the crunch.

In the first match in South Australia, South Adelaide easily accounted for the visitors 8.9 (57) to 4.7 (31).

The same result was expected when the Englishmen took the field against Port Adelaide on Tuesday, 10 July 1888. Hence the same crowd of just 2000 fans.

At the long break Port held a comfortable 19-point lead, 4.5 to 1.4. Even at three-quarter time it was still Port's game—7.5 (47) to 4.6 (30).

Then the whole character of the match changed. According to the *Observer*: 'For an hour the Englishmen were completely nonplussed by the little-marking of the Ports, who, however, took things easily. Then in the last quarter the Britishers went in like bulldogs and ran the proverbial rings around the seasiders. Such terrible fast play has seldom, if ever, been seen on the Adelaide Oval.'

It was left to a fellow who was later to become the first sportsman to captain England in both cricket and rugby, Andrew Stoddart, to kick the winning goal as the tourists shocked by taking the match 8.8 (56) to 7.8 (49). Stoddy, as he was known to teammates, was lauded by the *Observer* reporter: 'Such a brilliant forward as Stoddart ... has never been excelled by any local player. He simply ran past his men as though they were standing still.'

The Poms had beaten the locals at what was a truly alien game. They were to subsequently go down to Adelaide 6.13 (49) to 3.5 (23) and to Norwood 5.8 (38) to 3.1 (19). But no one could take away from them that historic one-off victory against Port Adelaide.

Sadly for the entrepreneurs they lost on the footy tour, too. This time they finished around £800 in the red.

And history would sadly show that two of those involved in that 'fluke' piece of sporting history at Adelaide Oval, Shewsbury and Stoddart, were both destined to commit suicide by putting a gun to their head and blowing their brains out—the former in 1903 and Stoddart in 1915.

Bertie the Carpet Snake Bites the Dust

It would not be an exaggeration to say that Bob Craig was one of the greatest all-round sportsmen Australia has known. He was a brilliant swimmer, winning eight NSW freestyle championships between 1899 and 1906 (although he was no match for his protégé, the great Barney Keiran, the first Aussie to break one minute for the 100 yards freestyle). Craig was also a fine water polo player (appearing in four Sydney Premiership-winning sides) and a real soccer star (helping Balmain to win the state's top event, the Gardiners' Cup, in 1905).

But it was on the rugby field that Craig really excelled. As an amateur he was one of the successes of the 1908–09 Wallabies side which toured Britain and North America. On this tour he played a Test against Wales and was in the Australian team that won the gold medal for rugby at the 1908 London Olympic Games. When he returned home, Craig was one of the 14 Wallabies to switch en masse to rugby league and he soon established himself in the professional code.

He played in three Test series against Britain, including one during the 1911–12 Kangaroo tour. On that visit Craig so impressed the directors of Aston Villa soccer club that they tried, in vain, to persuade him to stay in England for the famous team.

The big fella was an inveterate practical joker, with a dry, wicked sense of humour.

On the tour that netted him Olympic gold, Craig took Bertie, his pet carpet snake, with him in his bag. He wanted him along to keep him company and the pet duly obliged by curling up each night at the foot of Craig's bed. Bertie soon became a talking point as he was regularly let loose at cocktail parties to scare the women (and more often than not, the men).

Sadly, Britain proved much too cold for the pet carpet snake. Bertie died of pneumonia early on the tour and missed the celebrations for the team's Olympic gold medal win.

I'm Told You're a Footballer, Mr Barassi!

In the 1950s and '60s the press room at Sydney's Mascot Airport achieved a certain degree of notoriety. Not because of anything that was done there—be it known the most active pursuit was the almost constant game of cards. No, the notoriety came from the performances of the reptiles of the press—and one man in particular. To save his family from acute embarrassment, we'll call him Norman. After all, he was the person who inspired actor Garry McDonald to create the television character Norman Gunston.

Norman, who worked for one of the country's most influential newspapers, didn't realise what a buffoon he was. He was deadly serious when he came up with the string of legendary schoolboy howlers that embarrassed visiting celebrities. The celebs were wheeled into the press room, bleary-eyed after 12 or 15 hours winging their way across the Pacific or having spent the best of 30 hours on a cramped flight from the Old Dart with anything up to eight landings and takeoffs.

'Twas then that they were confronted by Norman. Hardly a daunting site at first. Norman, after all, was slight of build and well into middle age. It was when he proffered his first question that the look of amazement would spread over the victim's face.

'Now, just how many musicians do you have in your quartet, Mr Brubeck?'

'Mr Heston, it says here in the press release that you won an Oscar for your role in *Ben Hur*. This Oscar ... ummm. Does it carry much prestige with it?'

'I'm told that you are a British actor of some note, Mr Ustinov.'

'Your PR man tells me you're an entertainer, Mr Hope ... a comedian.'

To which Bob Hope dryly replied: 'I thought I was until I met you.'

'But I am being serious, Mr Hope.'

'Yes, you are. And that's what worries me.'

You may be wondering why Norman gets a mention in a book about sport. Well, it should be pointed out that, in the words of the old cliché, what Norman knew about sport could be written on the back of a postage stamp.

And so the questions he asked of famous sportsmen and women were, if it is at all possible, more bizarre than those that greeted the entertainers and politicians.

He knew not the difference between soccer, Aussie Rules and rugby league. For all he knew Lou Richards played for Balmain and Clive Churchill for Carlton. As for the wonderfully named soccer goalkeeper Norman Conquest ... he was probably confused with some foot-soldier of old.

Soccer superstar George Best made a visit.

'Mr Best, how well known are you in England?'

Then, when golfing legend Jack Nicklaus arrived ready to chalk up one his many Australian Open victories, our Norman was in his best form.

'Mr Nicklaus. You are a golfer. Do you make enough money to live on from golf, or do you have a second job?'

And what about the great cricket all-rounder Keith Miller, back from an Ashes tour of England?

'Thank you for your time. Now it's Keith Miller, isn't it. Can I just check the spelling of Miller?'

And, as a footnote, it should be pointed out that Norman, bless his little heart, put the same question to Frank Sinatra.

'Can I just check the spelling of Sinatra?'

Serving Up a Bit of Larry Dooley

When people would ask Larry O'Day, the old grappler of television's World Championship Wrestling days, how he spelled his surname, he would just give a shrug of the shoulders and stare at them with a quizzical look on his face.

'I haven't the slightest idea,' he would answer. 'Haven't a bloody clue. O'Day? O'Dea? Your guess is as good as mine.'

Before you started thinking the bloke who wrestled such celebrated figures as Killer Kowalski, Andre the Giant and Skull Murphy may have been thrown out of the ring and landed on his head too many times, or been rendered unconscious by too many sleeper holds, it has to be pointed out that O'Day (or O'Dea) was never the name on his driver's licence. It was Davies.

'When I had my first pro bout at the George's River Sailing Club in Sydney at the age of 16, the promoter wanted an Irish wrestler for his troupe,' he explained. 'There was a bloke called O'Day causing a bit of a brouhaha in the local council. So O'Day I became. Or O'Dea?

'People always thought I was an Irish Catholic when actually I was a Welsh Protestant. I wasn't Robinson Crusoe. My wrestling mate Ron Parker became Ron Miller only because he worked at a pub run by Miller's Brewery and he thought he might get some sponsorship.'

Now if you're like most of us and reckon wrestling is a fake, you wouldn't have got much argument from O'Day, even through the years when he promoted the sport ... um ... entertainment in Asia. It was there that once in the mid-1990s his grapplers drew a crowd of more than 30,000 to Indira Gandhi Stadium in New Delhi.

'It was different in my day,' he explained. 'There would be half-a-dozen genuine bouts early in each program before a couple of the clowns with gimmicks would roll around the ring in the main event.

'But even those clowns had learned the trade in the amateur ranks. Then it all changed. In the '80s and '90s the American promoters would go into gyms, grab a couple of body-builders filled with steriods and give them some gimmick.

'About all these so-called wrestlers could do was bounce off the ropes. And the bouts were over in three or four minutes because none of them was capable of wrestling for any longer than that.

'Back in the 1950s when I first started watching the sport they had just a couple of blokes with gimmicks—Gorgeous George and Chief Little Wolf. But both were accomplished wrestlers long before they decided to put on the war-paint.'

O'Day began in wrestling because at the time he saw it as one of the few sports in which he could earn some good money. Few footballers and cricketers in those days could earn a decent living from their chosen sport.

He had his first bout in 1960, telling everyone he was 18 (when in fact he was two years younger) so he was legally allowed inside the licensed clubs where most of the wrestling took place.

In 1964 he got his break when the Nine Network began weekend programs on wrestling with some of the biggest names in the world: Killer Kowalski, Waldo von Erich, Dominic De Nucci, Mario Milano, Spiros Arion.

The programs were unabashed commercials for the coming week's bouts at the capital city stadiums around Australia. They cost little to put on, rated well and helped boost the network's percentage of Australian content, as demanded by law.

Perhaps the most famous of all the wrestlers who filled stadiums around Australia was Killer Kowalski. He made headlines by disabling talk-show host Don Lane on camera with his claw hold. Lane had had the temerity to suggest the hold was a fake and paid the price.

'There was plenty of money to be made if you had a big name,' O'Day recalled. 'I remember seeing Killer's pay cheque for one night's wrestling. It was £2500 after tax. That was a fortune back in those days. At that time the average wage around Australia was around 50 quid a week.

'But Killer had been getting thousands a week for about 20 years.

'After he retired, a very rich man, he joined some obscure religious cult which fleeced him of all his money. From then on, Killer wandered around America, a derelict, knocking on the doors of the homes of old wrestlers begging for a meal or a few bucks to buy a drink.'

Others went mad or committed suicide.

'Brute Bernard and Skull Murphy took their own lives,' O'Day explained. 'Bernard hated black people and in a bar one night forced one to play Russian Roulette with him. They each had three turns and lived. Then on Bernard's fourth attempt he picked the chamber with the bullet.

'One wrestler threw himself off the top floor of the

Holiday Inn in Miami. I can't remember who that was.

'Yukon Eric was another. His wife walked out on him, so he went to the church where they had been married, sat on the steps, put a shotgun in his mouth and pulled the trigger.

'It was the drugs and booze that were the downfall of so many of my contemporaries. Steroids muddled many a brain . . . and coke and booze. I remember one bloke so high on acid that, when we were on a plane going from Perth to Sydney, he saw a moth and thought it was a vulture circling, waiting for him to die. The stewards had to tie him to his seat.

'Fritz von Erich's pain was different. His three sons committed suicide and his daughter died of a drug overdose.'

But other wrestlers became incredibly wealthy.

Lord James Blears, a regular on the Australian circuit in the 1950s, retired to live in luxury in Hawaii where he promoted surfing tournaments.

Andre the Giant wrestled almost to the day he died in the early 1990s.

He didn't need to. He was a rich man, owning a well-known restaurant in the Canadian city of Montreal and a 200-hectare property in the Blue Ridge Mountains in North Carolina. But he wrestled because the grapplers were the only friends he had.

'He thoroughly enjoyed himself when he was with other wrestlers—but deep down he hid an aching heart,' O'Day explained. 'He never had lasting, meaningful relationships with women—even though he longed for happiness. Everyone regarded him as a weirdo, something to be stared at.'

Because of his size—2.24 metres tall and weighing 235 kilograms—Andre had to travel first class. And O'Day remembered an incident when Andre, lonely up front, went to each of his fellow first-class passengers and asked if they would mind if he brought his mate (O'Day) up from tourist class.

LARRY O'DAY
'You did have to know how to wrestle'—Photo: Kewin Brown

'I ask you, who was going to argue with the big bloke?' said O'Day.

The Giant also had trouble getting taxi drivers willing to risk having him in their cabs.

'We used to hide him in hotel foyers,' recalls O'Day. 'As soon as the taxi driver opened the boot to stow our luggage, Andre would lumber out of hiding and plop himself in the taxi. The driver would go off his brain and we usually had to pay double the fare to placate him.'

Andre also had a giant thirst. He would regularly drink 60 stubbies in a sitting after a wrestling bout. Once, at Auckland Airport, he turned to O'Day and said: 'I hate this place, give me some of that anti-freeze you bought duty free.'

The 'anti-freeze' was Russian vodka. Andre emptied the bottle between the airport and his hotel and then went off in search of some beer chasers.

O'Day gave up wrestling at the age of 42.

But he did briefly come out of retirement a decade later when one of his team touring India and South-East Asia got into a spot of bother and had to leave town while the going was good.

'We were one short, so I pulled on the old wrestling trunks once again,' O'Day explained. 'I told the members of my troupe that if anyone hurt me, they would be on the next plane home. I was too old to suffer any unnecessary pain. I hadn't really wrestled seriously since the late 1970s. I was going downhill. You can kid other people for a while. But you can't kid yourself.'

Larry O'Day went to that great wrestling ring in the sky in 1997. He was only 53 years old. A few weeks before he passed away he was drinking with me and my photographer mate Kevin Brown in The Strand Hotel in Sydney's William Street. O'Day was as bold and brash as ever and fans were coming up to shake his oversized hand.

He told us: 'You know, I give thanks every day that, unlike so many of the other blokes, I am alive, sane and in one piece.'

Sadly, all that was about to change.

But we put to him the question everyone has wanted answered—were the wrestlers fair dinkum?

O'Day just smiled. 'Let's put it this way. You *did* have to know how to wrestle.'

French Farce at Flemington

There are plenty of furphies that have made it into sport's history books. Like the one about our first Olympic gold medallist Teddy Flack. Most journalists have written it—before we stopped and thought for a while.

The story was told that at Athens in 1896, when Flack won the 800 metres and 1500 metres, the Olympic organisers were so confused that they raised the Austrian flag and played the Austrian national anthem while Teddy was up on the dais.

Of course it's a furphy of the finest kind. It was five years before Federation and Australia didn't actually exist as a country. The good burghers of Athens raised the Union Jack and played God Save the Queen—because indeed Queen Victoria was on the throne at the time and we were a colony of Britain.

One of the other oft-repeated mistakes concerns the 1948 Melbourne Cup, won by the 80–1 outsider Rimfire. Browse through many racing books and newspaper articles and you will read how the win by jockey Ray Neville on Rimfire was the first and only success of his career.

Ripley would have loved it. 'Believe It Or Not'. I would

be willing to bet that come November and this story will be trotted out yet again. Believe It Or Not? Don't you believe it! Neville *had* won a race before the Melbourne Cup. Just one, mind you, at Flemington six weeks earlier on a galloper called Lincoln. And he was to win a handful of races after the Cup. But just a handful.

Yet the Melbourne Cup of 1948 proves that fairytales *can* come true. That dreams *can* become reality. That flukes *do* happen. Just ask Ray Neville!

He was a kid from the Mallee district of Victoria. From Birchip to be exact. Along the Sunraysia Highway on the way to Mildura—although it probably wasn't called the Sunraysia Highway in those days when it was just a dusty, pot-holed track like the rest of the country roads.

Ray was a 15-year-old kid who was apprenticed to top Melbourne trainer Lou Robertson at Aspendale down on the foreshores of Port Phillip Bay near Mordialloc.

At the time of the 1948 Cup, Neville had only been riding for about two months. He'd picked up one winner at Flemington. But quite frankly, if you were one of the connections of a Melbourne Cup starter, you wouldn't in your wildest dreams give him a ride in the big one. Except Stan Boyden, the trainer of Rimfire, did!

Rimfire's owner didn't want to run his horse in the big race. And who could blame him? Rimfire was a real crock. Okay, so he had run third in the Brisbane Cup the previous year to Blue Boots and Russia. And considering Russia had won the Melbourne Cup that wasn't bad form.

But Rimfire had done in one of his legs during the Brisbane Cup. The leg was still unsound and he'd broken down three months earlier. Oh, yes. Rimfire also suffered from chronic saddle-sores. And he'd pulled up lame after jockey WA Smith rode him into sixth place in the Hotham Handicap on the Saturday before the Cup. Hardly the best preparation for Australia's greatest horse race.

That Rimfire recovered was a tribute to Boyden's ability. He kept applying hot and cold compresses to Rimfire's leg for 48 hours after the Hotham. He did so because he had had a dream that Rimfire would win on the first Tuesday in November.

The fact that the owner Guy Raymond, a VCR committeeman and part-owner of the famous St Albans Stud near Bendigo, agreed to let Rimfire run is tribute to the powers of persuasion by Boyden.

Neville was originally going to Flemington as strapper for another horse in the Cup, the 100–1 outsider Westralian. Robertson thought it was better not to tell him about his mount in the big race until the Tuesday morning. Didn't want to get the kid too excited.

It was 4 am that he first spoke to Neville: 'Get your work done quickly and clean your gear. You have a ride in the Cup. It's on the outsider Rimfire.'

Neville had never seen the horse before, let alone ridden him. It was like something out of a French farce at Flemington.

Neville was pint-sized, to say the least.

Rimfire's silks were way too large. Robertson tightened Neville's jodhpurs with a safety pin to make sure the tail of the silks wouldn't come out. Indeed the tail came down to Neville's knees. In years to come, Robertson was to laugh: 'More was sat on than could be seen.'

The sleeves were so long that they had to be rolled up and further safety pins used to keep them from interfering with Neville's hands. He certainly didn't look the part.

It mattered not. Neville was ready for the big occasion.

The youngster quietly worked Rimfire through the field. He trailed the well-credentialled Dark Marne and three furlongs from home readied Rimfire to go past two other fancied horses, Vagabond and Royal Scot.

The 4–1 favourite Howe (ridden by Harold Badger) looked set to run over him, but suddenly veered out almost at right angles, having broken down in the near fetlock. Jack Thompson on Dark Marne went after Rimfire. And the two horses went stride for stride over the final furlong. They hit the line as one and the photo gave it to Rimfire.

It was the first time that the photo-finish had ever been used to decide the winner of the Melbourne Cup. Dark Marne's owner Tom Cooke noted: 'I thought I had won. But the camera which is, or should be, dead on the line, said "No". I can't argue with that.'

Did the camera lie? Some weeks later it was moved. According to the VCR this was just 'minor adjustments'.

'I won the race alright,' said Neville years later. 'They keep talking a lot of bullshit about it. But I won. I knew Dark Marne was challenging so I rode Rimfire as hard as I could. On the post I knew I had won.'

As for the VRC's 'minor adjustments': 'They didn't make any difference to my result.'

After the Cup it was business as usual for Neville. He looked after Westralian on the float back to Robertson's stable. His winning percentage was £475, with owner Raymond rounding it up to £500. That night Neville was given a larger plate of steak and eggs than normal at a special celebration dinner. And he was then allowed to go to Wirth's Circus where he was presented with a gold-mounted whip, the trophy given annually by the Wirth family to the winning jockey. The next day he celebrated his sixteenth birthday.

It was virtually Neville's last hurrah.

Increasing weight forced him out of the business within a year and he began a career as a carpenter. Rimfire never won another race.

Neville tried a comeback in 1963, riding over the jumps and managed a handful of winners at places like Apsley and Donald in Victoria. His last success was in November that year in an insignificant hurdle race at Ballarat on a horse called Solitude.

It was a long way from Flemington on the first Tuesday in November 1948.

Two Hat-Tricks... Yeah, Yeah

For so many Australians, cricket was never watched at the MCG, the SCG or the Gabba. It was heard on the ABC. The solid tones of the likes of Alan McGilvray, Bernie Kerr or Clive Harburg. And the reasoned summaries by Johnny Moyes.

Moyes was like Moses. He spoke ... and you listened and believed.

So when Moyes reckoned that Tommy Matthews had only average ability 'in all departments' you reasoned that Tommy was a dud. Even if Tommy had died a year before you had even been born. God ... or at least his right-hand man ... had spoken. Dud he must have been.

But then the doubts crept in. If he was such a dud, why was he in the record books? The only man in Test cricket history to have snared two hat-tricks in the same match ... and on the same day.

Matthews, it transpired, was a useful batsman who bowled medium pace, throwing in the occasional spell of spin. A googly or two. But, sadly, not much more.

The selectors were looking for a consistent all-rounder when they came to choose the Aussie side to tour England in 1912. Matthews fitted the bill. He did his job to the best of his ability on tour and as a result found himself in the Test side to play the Old Trafford match against South Africa in the triangular series that also involved England.

It was on 28 May that he made his name. In the first innings Matthews dismissed the last three South Africans in successive balls. Rolland Beaumont was bowled for 38. And Sid Pegler and Tommy Ward both fell leg before wicket for a duck.

The South Africans followed on. And eventually the Aussie captain Syd Gregory threw the ball to Matthews in the hope that he would again clean up the innings. He sure did! Herbie Taylor was bowled for 21, Reggie Schwartz caught and bowled for nought. And poor old Ward, the wicketkeeper? He was caught and bowled for a duck. What is it they called it? A king pair! Ward could never live it down.

Matthews took only 10 other wickets during his Test career. Was the Manchester performance a fluke? Um . . . we hesitate to use the advertising slogan made famous by another Aussie Test-playing Matthews. But probably . . . yeah, yeah!

The Greatest Ego of All

They called him the Voice of Football. The Greatest Name of All in the Greatest Game of All. George Lovejoy.

The fans either loved him or they hated him. There was most definitely no middle ground. Around Bundaberg, where he grew up and his dad ruled the rugby league game with an iron fist, they revered him as if he was a god. At Ipswich he was reviled as a disciple of the Devil.

'Yes. Some of the fans, especially those out at Ipswich, gave me a bit of stick in my time,' said George with a wry grin. 'But everything I said in 33 years of broadcasting

GEORGE LOVEJOY
A meeting of two legendary Rugby League commentators—Australia's George Lovejoy (left) and Britain's Eddie Waring (right).

football . . . well, if I had my time over again I wouldn't change a word. Not a single word!

'Of course, I was often accused of saying things I didn't. One player at Ipswich didn't speak to me for a quarter of a century because someone told him that during a broadcast I had called him "a filthy animal". In fact, I had said that when he tackled one of his opponents he was like a beast of prey pouncing on a terrified victim. He probably still believes I had maligned him.'

Two decades after his last regular football broadcast, George Lovejoy was a very different person. He was more relaxed and obviously enjoyed the leisurely lifestyle that comes with retirement from one's day job. But the ego was still there. Some say it was the biggest in rugby league. And you would never find George disagreeing.

'When you know what you're talking about ... and you know you're right ... why make excuses?' was the way he always put it.

Why indeed! There was no chance of stopping him once he tucked the ball under his arms and was off and running—in a manner of speaking.

Indeed, there was rarely any chance of stopping him—from the moment, as a four-year-old, George Lovejoy began singing in front of the grandstand at the West Bundaberg Recreation Grounds (now Salter Oval). His reward for this half-time entertainment was a cap full of pennies and lollies.

'I had a repertoire of just three songs,' he recalled. 'There were two about the great pioneer aviator Bert Hinkler and one to the tune of "The Road to Gundagai". What most people don't know is that the song was originally "On the Road to Bundaberg". But the music publishers wanted more Aboriginal-sounding words in it. So the Bernard River became the Murrumbidgee and so on. I was very upset as Bernard is my middle name.'

You don't know whether to believe him. But it's a good story, nevertheless.

'My sister was Bert Hinkler's secretary,' he continued. 'One of my wonderful memories is of Bert taking me to see the plane he flew from England and sitting me in its cockpit. It was stuck in Bert's garage, with the wings folded up.'

George was later mascot and ball-boy for the local rugby league team. Not because he was any good at sport. It was because his dad was the president of the club. It's not what you know, it's who you know!

He got his start in radio just after World War II as an announcer/advertising salesman on 4BU, Bundaberg.

The nation's sports broadcaster was a fellow called Verdi Stibe.

'All the Stibe family were named after classical composers, although Verdi's brothers changed them to common or garden names. For example, Puccini Stibe called himself Percy,' George explained. 'Colin Stibe was one of three Bundaberg players in the Queensland Sheffield Shield side—the others were the Test cricketer Don Tallon and his brother Bill.

'I can remember Bill saying back in 1936 that the only way Queensland would ever win the Sheffield Shield was if they raffled the bloody thing and Queensland bought all the tickets. How prophetic! Well, they did eventually win it. But it took another 60-odd years.

'Verdi was a cripple with stumps instead of legs. He used to walk around on his hands, wearing an old pair of Don Tallon's wicket-keeping gloves.'

Eventually Verdi retired. And George stepped in to call the football.

He never looked back. In 1949 he moved to Brisbane to join 4BH as an advertising executive. And the following year he began broadcasting the Brisbane Premiership.

'My style was different. It was controversial and the public was soon talking about me,' he recalled. 'At the start I didn't deliberately set out to be controversial. But when I saw it was working I did. I probably annoyed the purists. But I got a lot of people who knew nothing about rugby league listening.'

So many, that at one stage he had the highest listening audience, per capita, of any football caller in Australia. In one period of almost 20 years he called 652 games for 4BH without missing a single match through illness or any other reason. It is believed to be a world record for a radio caller in any major sport. And, until the proliferation of new stations in the past few decades, he had the distinction of having at least one of his football calls being broadcast by every commercial station in Queensland.

He made no secret of where his allegiances lay. With Queensland and Australia!

'I didn't favour any club,' he was always quick to point out. 'But when it came to interstate matches I was a Queenslander through and through. We Queenslanders have been accused of being parochial. No, it's the Sydney mob that must wear that tag.

'You know, back in 1959 we won three of the four interstate matches. But when it came to picking the 26-man Kangaroo squad to tour England and France there were only eight Queenslanders chosen. It was a disgrace. We should have had at least 13, possibly more. That was one of the lowest acts in the history of rugby league.'

Twice Lovejoy was involved in controversial broadcasts from outside football grounds.

The first was at Ipswich when the locals became so incensed with his opinions of the Ipswich side that they banned him from the arena. So he broadcast from the roof of a house overlooking the ground ('The drabbest ground in Australia').

He picked out one house, but the owner refused, explaining that he was a shop steward at the railway workshops 'and the boys would lynch me if I let you'. But the shop steward suggested George talk to his next-door neighbour, who just happened to be the shop steward's daughter and a Lovejoy fan.

In more recent years he joined Billy J Smith in a tower erected adjacent to Lang Park and on the roofs of houses overlooking suburban grounds after 4IP was given exclusive rights to Brisbane football and commentators from the other stations were shut out of the grounds.

Lovejoy also recalled a feat that he reckoned must rank as one of the real Australian sporting oddities. One year he broadcast a match from Toowoomba for two opposition Brisbane stations. On 4BK the call was sponsored by Bulimba

Beer. On 4BH the sponsor was the Queensland Temperance Union.

And he admitted to being tongue-tied in one major sporting call. It was a championship tennis match at the famous Milton courts in Brisbane in the early 1950s. On one side of the net was a doubles combination of Lew Hoad and Ken Rosewall and on the other Rex Hartwig and Mervyn Rose.

'Tennis is so fast that you can't call every shot in a singles match, let alone the doubles,' he noted. 'And here I was with two Hs, Hoad and Hartwig, and two almost identical names, Rose and Rosewall. It was a nightmare.'

But rugby league always has been George's real love. And largely thanks to his broadcasts it's become the true love of a couple of generations of Queenslanders.

There is one thing about which George will hear no argument—the greatest league player.

'There can be only one choice—Wally Lewis,' he said. 'Until Wally came along I thought Johnny Raper was the greatest Australian footballer and Duncan Hall the greatest Queenslander. But not any more.'

And what about the Coca-Cola seller who used to wander past his broadcasting box in the old days, the call of 'Get your Coca-Cola. Icy cold Coke' drowning out even George's majestic call a couple of times every match.

'People would tell me that when they were at the match they were never satisfied until they had seen the boy walk past me,' George said with a chuckle. 'Of course, they were fibbing. He didn't exist. The voice was a tape recording of my young son who is now middle aged. And back in the studio, they'd turn down my call and play the tape at quiet moments during the afternoon. There never was a Coke seller.'

And, of course, Coca-Cola never paid for the interruptions. Perish the thought!

Come in Spinner

What odds to these embarrassments? Author David Clark, researching a book on cricket curiosities, reckons he feels sorry for Australian off-spinner Gavin Robertson. The cricketer suffered the indignity of having the first ball he bowled in a limited-overs international hit for six. Sri Lanka's Arjuna Ranatunga was the batsman responsible, at Saravanamuttu Stadium in Colombo on 13 September 1994.

If that wasn't enough, English batsman Graeme Hick hit a six off the first ball Robertson bowled in an international on *home* soil. Hick's six came at the Melbourne Cricket Ground on 10 January 1995.

And then there's Aussie fast bowler and recognised rabbit, Glenn McGrath. He was dismissed off the first ball he received in his Test debut (versus New Zealand at the WACA Ground in Perth on 13 November 1993) and in his one-day international debut (against South Africa at the MCG on 9 December 1993).

But isn't that what fans pay money to go to watch?

'Gelignite' Jack's Perfect Drive

Some cynics suggest the following anecdote was no more than a figment of the fertile imagination of a freelance journalist in need of a quid. But it has become part of Australian folklore and, as such, deserves to be repeated here.

Let's set the scene. It was July 1954 and some 246 cars were racing their way around Australia in the second of the famous Redex Reliability Trials. They'd reached Townsville in north Queensland where the showground had been turned into the official checkpoint for the competitors. Jack Murray, one of the best-known names in Australian motor racing, was waiting near the grandstand for his turn to be flagged off on the next leg of the rally.

Bored with the wait, he wandered across to a nearby tin toilet and shoved a stick of gelignite under the rickety outhouse, attached a long fuse, lit said fuse and strolled back to his car.

Suddenly there was an explosion and every head turned in the direction of the blast, just in time to see the toilet falling apart, and a startled former occupant struggling away, trousers around his ankles.

Murray shrugged his shoulders: 'He musta gone into the dunny after I lit the fuse. But the only thing that's hurt is his pride.'

The gelignite was part of Murray's tools of trade. He packed it together with his spanners and spare parts on each and every one of the rallies in which he competed. It was his

'GELIGNITE' JACK MURRAY

trademark—so much so that to this day almost half a century after some of his greatest victories he is remembered as 'Gelignite' Jack Murray.

More about the Redex Trial later.

The Melbourne-born Murray was a great all-round sportsman, a Victorian junior cycling champion, an RAN lightweight boxing champion and the winner of the Australian amateur welterweight wrestling titles for five straight years from 1930 to 1934. He won the first Sydney–Newcastle–Sydney ocean race for speedboats in 1964. And he, and another great name in sport, motor racing's 'Wild Bill' McLachlan, are recognised as having introduced the first organised water-skiing to Australia, in 1946.

However, it was in motor sport that Murray became a household name.

He was a qualified motor mechanic who, with his brother Ray, started what was eventually to be a thriving motor workshop in Sydney in 1934. They poured the profits into the purchase of taxis and eventually owned a large fleet which gave them a bit of spending money.

Around 1942 Jack Murray bought a Mackellar Special racing car. It was unwanted by others because it had crashed in a race at Penrith in 1939, killing three spectators and injuring 39 others. In this car Murray finished fifth in the 1945 Australian Grand Prix, setting the record for the fastest lap during the race.

He then switched to a Day Special, which had a Ford V8 engine mounted in a Bugatti chassis, winning many races including the 1948 Bathurst Grand Prix on the Mt Panorama track.

But by this stage he was dabbling in water-skiing on the Hawkesbury River north of Sydney. As is the normal custom he was towed behind speedboats. But on at least one occasion he is said to have reached higher speeds by using a low-flying light aircraft to tow him along the river.

In the early 1950s, English businessman Reg Shepherd, who was a high-flyer with the company that sold Redex oil additive, decided on a foolproof way to publicise his product. He spent £10,000—a lot of money in those days—to organise Australia's most gruelling car rally. The Redex 'Round Australia Reliability Trial' wasn't quite what the name suggested—it did not include Western Australia (although later trials did) but it attracted enormous media coverage.

Jack Murray decided to enter in a brand new Chrysler-Plymouth. On Sunday, 30 August 1953, with co-driver and navigator Bill Murray (no relation), he was one of the 186 entrants cheered away from the Sydney Showground by 200,000 enthusiastic onlookers.

All went according to plan until a so-called 'horror stretch' between Townsville and Mt Isa. This horror stretch had been introduced in case of a possible count-back at the finish. If such a count-back were to be necessary the result would be determined by the times on this leg.

With so much at stake, the drivers tried hard—some too hard. Fifteen cars crashed, six so badly that they were left where they were to rust. One of the 15 was the Murrays' Chrysler-Plymouth, which had swerved to avoid a bullock near Cloncurry and rolled over. But Jack Murray still found time to joke about his plight. The car was resting on its roof with the wheels still spinning when the next competitor arrived on the scene. As he pulled up, Murray shouted: 'We're all right. But have you got a ring spanner? Nine-sixteenths.'

The other driver looked puzzled: 'What the hell do you need a ring spanner for?'

'Well,' Gelignite Jack replied. 'I thought I might adjust the brakes while the wheels were up like this!'

Murray was out of the race and had no need for the gelignite he carried. He said it was to clear any fallen trees or stray rocks out of his way. But some critics cruelly suggested he used it to blow up the road behind him to make things harder for his opposition.

The pair was back for the following year's Redex Trial. This was longer and much more gruelling. But Murray had learned a lot from his first effort. He decided to drive a 1947 Canadian Ford Deluxe V8, affectionately known as 'The Grey Ghost'. He chose the second-hand car, which had already driven 120,000 kilometres, because of its high clearance off the ground.

The two Murrays made the 15,500 kilometre journey around the continent without a loss of a single penalty point to claim the £2000 winner's cheque. Only 130 of the 246 cars that started made it to the finish at the Sydney Showground, where 30,000 screaming fans were waiting. When the Murrays arrived, they were mobbed and it took 15 minutes for them to ease their car through the throng into the arena.

The pair spoke to the crowd standing on the bonnet of The Grey Ghost. Gelignite Jack told them the only damage to the car was two broken shock absorber links, damaged on the Cloncurry–Mt Isa horror stretch.

Bill Murray said they sometimes had to drive at speeds of 80 miles per hour (130 kilometres/hour) to make up for lost time and to avoid losing penalty points. He said the run across the Snowy Mountains the previous day had been the most difficult.

'Coming down Talbingo Mountain at 50 miles per hour (80 kilometres/hour) our brakes failed from overheating and we had to use the gears as brakes,' he said. 'We arrived at the next control with only a minute to spare.'

It was later revealed that a gamble by Jack Murray almost cost them victory. Heading for Broome, in the north of Western Australia, he decided not to take a time-wasting detour to refuel the Ford. He had miscalculated and the car ran out of petrol 50 kilometres from Broome. Bill Murray grabbed a petrol can and headed off down the road where he came across another competitor in a Holden that had broken down. The two crews did a deal. The Holden would hand over petrol in return for a tow into Broome. Thus, the Murrays were able to reach the next checkpoint on time.

Jack Murray was running third in the last of the Redex Trials (in 1955), but he forced officials to disqualify him by not checking in at the finish in protest against a 'horror stretch' through a swamp near Canberra. The Redex hero took part in several Ampol Trials (successors to the Redex events) but broken axles and navigational errors kept him out of the prizemoney.

By the 1960s he had a new obsession. He constructed a special kite that was strapped to his back and when water-skiing would lift him off the water and into the air. He called it an aquacopter. But at his first attempt it collapsed when he was 30 metres airborne. He crashed back into the water, luckily without any serious injury.

On another occasion he used a powerboat in an attempt to tow the famous hang-glider, Bill 'The Birdman' Moyes, from Sydney to the Gold Coast. Off Forster the boat hit some flotsam and began to sink. Moyes glided down and the pair managed to pull the crippled boat ashore.

In 1964, Gelignite Jack and co-driver Keith Whitehead drove Murray's speedboat *Tact* to victory in the 257 kilometre Sydney–Newcastle–Sydney race, winning by an impressive 57 minutes. They tried to repeat the win a year later, but when well in front on the return journey off Norah Heads they hit a whale.

Age never stopped Murray. He was 59 when he teamed up with respected motoring writer and television commentator Evan Green to compete unsuccessfully in the London to Sydney car rally. Four years later the pair competed, again without success, in the London to Mexico City World Cup Rally.

In 1980, blood circulation problems forced surgeons to amputate Murray's right leg. It didn't dim his spirits: 'They've removed my pin. But hell, it's only a leg. It's not the bloody end of everything.'

But the end was not far away. On 11 December 1983, Murray died of a heart attack in Sydney's St Vincent's Hospital. One obituary pointed out: 'It just won't be the same without him!' And it wasn't.

Not So Gay Gordon

Edward De Bono would have a field day trying to work out how schoolteachers think. Lateral thinking? Perish the thought.

Here I was in Monaro High School at Cooma, the headquarters of the Snowy Mountains Scheme. We had no regular sporting competition with other schools—the nearest being two hours or more drive away.

So we had *Houses*. A throwback to the public school system of England.

Only our Houses had to have an Australian flavour. And even though they were created for sporting competition there would be no mention of sporting heroes. No Don Bradman. No Boy Charlton. No John Landy. Especially, no Marjorie Jackson. Women in sport? Hardly!

Poets were the order of the day at Monaro High School.

Paterson. Yep, we all knew about Banjo, especially there in the foothills of the Snowy Mountains where men were men and mountains were there to be conquered.

Lawson? Hey, what about the loaded dog? A good sporting yarn if ever there was one.

Kendall? Now, that taxed our memory. I was slotted into Kendall House. To this day I haven't read a word of his poems ... much to my embarrassment. I suspect he was pretty good.

And Gordon? Now you're talking about sportsmen.

Once again, I've never liked much of what Gordon wrote. But it is said that as a bush balladeer he paved the way for

NOT SO GAY GORDON   85

the likes of Paterson and Kendall. Maybe even for Lawson ... although I'm sure it was Henry's mum who was his guiding influence.

But I digress.

Gordon. He was a jump jockey. A bloody good jump jockey, if records are anything to go by.

Even today, if you pick up *Millers Guide*, the bible of racing, you will find that Adam Lindsay Gordon rode three steeplechase winners at Flemington on 10 October 1868. It was the first time this had ever happened. And in the intervening century and a bit it has happened only twice again. No mean feat.

For those who like to dwell on trivia, and I am one of them, Gordon's winners were Babbler, Viking and Cadger. So there!

It is said that if you read Gordon's writing and digest it closely you will realise that here was a lonely soul. A man racked by self-doubt. Sad in the extreme.

In early 1870 he published a book of verse, *Bush Ballads and Galloping Rhymes*. Kendall loved the book and wrote in glowing terms about it.

But after a fall in a steeplechase Gordon became quite melancholic. On the morning of 24 June 1870, he crept out of bed and walked down to Brighton Beach on Port Phillip Bay and blew his brains out.

Any Port in a Storm

What is it about the Australian bush that produces so many characters? Larger than life figures that even a Hollywood scriptwriter would not dare dream up.

Many have achieved legendary status. Blokes like bushie jackeroo RM Williams, who lent his name to a whole range of clothing. Poor farmers' son Hugh McKay who invented the Sunshine Harvester because he was sick and tired of harvesting the crops by hand. Pop Kaisler, who back in the 1920s built the world's first campervan.

And gun shearer Jacky Howe who, in 1892, sheared 327 merino sheep in 7 hours and 20 minutes—using hand blades. That's around one sheep every 80 seconds. Howe, of course, gave his name to the working man's blue singlet.

Now Col Hodges would never in his wildest dreams dare to suggest he was worthy of even wiping the boots of Jacky Howe. But he's dabbled in shearing for most of his adult life.

He's also a racetrack caller. But shearing is in the blood of this country character who's lived most of his life around the central-west of New South Wales, but whose employment as a shearer has taken him from Victoria right up into the centre of Queensland.

Wherever there was work.

'It's been nigh on 30 years now. I keep threatening to retire,' he says. 'Many a time I've decided I've had enough and gone close to throwing all my shearing gear into the river. But at the last minute I shake my head and shove it back in the boot of my car.

'It's my insurance against poverty.'

Hodges also loves the camaraderie of shearing.

'Shearers are good, honest people,' he says. 'You hear about Aussie mateship. Well, it's there for all to see in the shearing fraternity. Shearers never let their mates down.

'They never take a sickie—you have to be on death's doorstep before you'd let your mates down.

'There was a scientific study done by some university bloke in South Australia a few years ago. It concluded that shearing was the hardest physical job in the world.

'It's true. Mate, at the end of the day even your hair aches.'

Hodges tells the story of one team who went to a job out near Lake Cargelligo in south-western New South Wales.

On the way the car carrying two of the blokes crashed and caught fire.

They were badly burned but still worked for three days until the pain eventually forced them off to hospital.

Hodges remembers it well.

He explains how the 'two old rascals' got out of the crash okay, but one of them shouted at the other to get the port out of the boot of the burning car.

His mate rushed back and grabbed a suitcase.

'No, not that port. I meant the other port,' the first bloke shouted as he grabbed a flagon of McWilliams Royal Reserve Port and got burned for his troubles.

Hodges is just one in a thousand when it comes to shearing.

But he is well known as a racecaller on Sky Channel and the network of racing radio stations around Australia.

He became something of a minor celebrity in January 1997, when he called a triple dead-heat at a country meeting at Cowra. It was only the fourth triple dead-heat since photo-finish cameras were introduced in Australia half a century ago.

'It didn't mean much to me,' he explains. 'It was just

another race. But the next day all these breakfast radio announcers started calling from as far away as Perth and north Queensland.

'I called it right, too. As they hit the line I bellowed "it's almost a three-way dead heat".

'I couldn't have cared less. I had backed the horse that finished fourth, a neck away from the winners.'

Hodges called his first race when he was just eight years old.

He was at a one-teacher primary school at Gunning Gap, north of Canberra. Just 25 kids.

The boys cleared a dusty trotting track. The luckless girls were the horses and the boys would harness them with imitation reins fashioned from rope. They'd then run behind the girls as 'drivers'.

Hodges teamed up with the fastest girl, who was handicapped to start from 36 yards behind the slowest team.

'That way I could see what was happening as I called the races,' he remembers. 'One day things got a bit hectic and a few of us used some whips made from branches of pepper trees to whack the girls' legs to make them run faster.

'That was the end of our trotting meetings. And all the boys got the cane—six of the best.'

At Forbes High School he also ran an SP service, taking from fellow pupils bets from one penny to a couple of shillings. Well, he did until he went broke after he gave one kid odds of 25–1 on the 1964 Melbourne Cup winner Polo Prince.

He also had a failed attempt at bookmaking as an adult, getting into trouble with the authorities when, in an attempt to strum up business, he employed two young ladies in bikinis to be his pencilers (the assistants who would write down all the bets).

Hodges became a real-life race caller when, between shifts as a shearer, he helped out a friend Bobby Gunn who was ill. Gunn died and Hodges took over his job.

These shifts include the most unusual race meeting in the world—the once-a-year Port Vila Charity Cup Day in Vanuatu for which the Pacific and International Travel Centre books a couple of planeloads of Australian tourists.

For 364 days a year the racetrack on the outskirts of the Vanuatu capital is a cow paddock. The day before the races in July the cows are herded away and the racetrack constructed.

Everything from the rails to the horse-boxes are made from bamboo, freshly harvested for the big race day. The morning after the races are over, everything is burned to the ground and the cattle return to graze.

Horses go round with such names as Fine Cotton (not the infamous ring-in of the same name), Another Westpac Folly, Horse and Equus. Jockeys are known only by Christian names (which sometimes change during the afternoon).

One year a horse called Spook won a couple of races.

The Ni-Vanuatu (the local people) are a superstitious lot and they were convinced the horse was literally spooked—possessed by spirits.

Hodges explains how the following year a couple of the owners brought in a local medicine man to rid the racecourse of any evil spirits and to ensure their horses won.

It is part of local folklore that, on the morning of the races, the witch-doctor drank a bit too much of the local kava and got his riding instructions a bit mixed up.

Spook most definitely did not win. But neither did the horses of the owner who had employed him.

'Ah, racing in Vanuatu,' sighs Hodges. 'Wouldn't miss it for quids.'

The End of an Innings

Victorian cricketer RW 'Dick' Wardill holds a cherished spot in the history of Australian cricket. In December 1867, he scored 110 against New South Wales. No other batsman had previously scored a century in first-class cricket in Australia.

Wardill was also one of the figures behind the establishment of the Victorian Cricketers' Association, the body responsible for conducting the early intercolonial matches.

Sadly, Wardill is also remembered for another reason. As one of the VCA hierarchy, he was negotiating with the legendary English cricketer Dr WG Grace to bring a team to Australia. But Wardill never lived to see his tour plans come to fruition. On 17 August 1873, he committed suicide by jumping into the Yarra River in Melbourne. He was distressed after being caught embezzling £7000 from his employer, the Victorian Sugar Company, to cover gambling debts.

Lou the Lip Never Lost His Zip

You only have to meet Lou Richards to understand why the National Trust once listed him as one of Australia's Living Treasures.

His face is as roughly hewn as many of those facades of old buildings that have been preserved for future generations to view with wonder. His voice is unlike any other. Rasping. Dissonant. Inharmonious in the extreme. But his enthusiasm for sport—Australian football in particular—is infectious.

The National Trust bestowed its honour on Lou in 1982.

It was a great period for the footy star turned media legend.

Within a period of 12 months he was also named King of Moomba, a great honour in the city by the Yarra, and the Queen awarded him the MBE.

The MBE was front-page news and inspired one reader of the Melbourne *Sun* newspaper to wax lyrically:

> 'We wondered how Liz
> Could choose for our Lou
> A gong to which he could really aspire.
> We were all in a tizz
> Til we finally knew
> He's the Mouth of the British Empire.'

The Mouth of the British Empire helped inspire his beloved

Collingwood to the VFL Premiership in 1953. He was captain of the 'Pies and that grand final was one of the best of his 250 games with the club.

He quit the football field three years later. It was two weeks before the final playoffs. Richards, although skipper, reckoned his form had slumped so much that he didn't deserve a spot in the top team. Unselfishly, he hung up his boots.

The former toothpaste-tube maker had begun a media career within days of his quitting football. He was asked to write for the now-defunct *Argus* newspaper and then later the *Sun*. Radio followed and finally television.

He was regularly on the box from almost the day the first television pictures were beamed into Australian homes back in the late 1950s. For years it was with Channel 7 in Melbourne on the long-running 'World of Sport' program and the Saturday footy telecasts that were beamed around Australia. Later it was with the Nine Network's 'Wide World of Sports'. His three decades in television was a record for an Australian sports broadcaster.

'My old radio mentor Doug Elliott taught me that the most important thing was to be yourself,' Lou recalled. 'In showbiz it was a must if you wanted to succeed and stay successful. And television sport always was most certainly showbiz.'

Lou's media life was crammed with incidents and characters that in another era would have been fodder for the likes of famous American author Damon Runyon.

Like the fun Richards had writing his weekly football previews for the *Sun*, giving his predictions that were quickly dubbed 'The Kiss of Death', and bestowing on footballers nicknames the like of which had never been seen before.

In some of his previews (he wrote about 4200 of them) Lou gave a Collingwood player called Con Britt the nickname Edgar. The original Edgar Britt, a fine jockey who rode with success in Britain, has a special place in Australian folklore as unwittingly lending his name to the rhyming slang for a bodily function we all have to perform regularly every day. It took the newspaper editor several months before he realised the significance of footballing Britt's nickname.

Another time Lou was on a celebrity speaking engagement in a Victorian country town. With him was ex-jockey Peter Bakos, himself a raconteur of some note.

'We were staying in the same pub,' Lou recalled. 'I walked into his room and saw him shaving. He was standing in the washbasin so he could see in the mirror.

'I love jockeys. They make me feel so tall.'

Then there was the time he met world heavyweight boxing legend Muhammad Ali. It was at the Woolloomooloo Police Boys' Club in Sydney.

As the champ alighted from his limo, Lou jumped out and shook his hand. Then he brazenly told Ali: 'Don't wash your hand. You can tell them all back home in the States that this is the hand that shook Lou Richards' hand.'

Ali was bewildered.

'I get paid for being a fool, what's your reason?' he asked Richards.

The reply was immediate: 'Okay, Ali, you've got the same old lip, but you're losing your zip.'

At which the champ burst out laughing and grabbed Lou in a bear hug. The picture of the encounter holds pride of place on the mantelpiece in Richards' Melbourne home.

As he was apt to point out, they didn't call him Lou the Lip for nothing.

Going for the Doctor

It was really a fluke that Sammy Woods played Test cricket for Australia. Not that he didn't deserve to. He was acknowledged as a fine all-round sportsman, as his record shows. It is just the circumstances surrounding his selection are unique, as is the fact that he had never played first-class cricket in Australia before representing his country of birth at Test level.

Woods, born in the Sydney suburb of Ashfield in 1867 and educated at Sydney Grammar (where he is said to have once taken seven wickets with successive deliveries), went to England to complete his education at Brighton College and Cambridge University. At Cambridge he made a name for himself at billiards, soccer and, especially cricket and rugby union. On the rugby field, Woods, a tall, strapping lock-forward, was capped 13 times for England.

When the Australian cricket team, captained by Percy McDonnell, toured England in 1888 there was a shortage of good bowlers. This was because the great all-rounder George Griffen had refused to tour and the fact that Sam Jones was cut down by smallpox. McDonnell turned to Woods to bolster the ranks of the Australians in the three Tests (at Lord's, The Oval and Old Trafford). Sadly, he didn't show his true worth for Australia, bowling only 54 overs, with his five wickets costing 24.20 apiece. And his six innings reaped only 32 runs (at an average of 5.33). He was twice dismissed for a duck.

But it was not the end of Woods' Test career. He was to become one of only five players to play Tests for both

Australia and the Mother Country when chosen to tour South Africa in 1895–96 with Lord Hawke's English side, scoring a half-century at Johannesburg.

Woods was also known for his quick wit. Once, while playing for Somerset he clean-bowled the great Dr WG Grace. Now, Grace was known for his penchant of refusing to acknowledge umpires' decisions giving him out. This time it was cut and dried, but as Grace departed for the pavilion, Woods is said to have quipped: 'I shouldn't go, doctor. There is still one stump standing!'

The Million Dollar Mermaid

So you reckon synchronised swimming isn't really a sport? You would have got short shrift from Annette Kellerman had you ever suggested that to her. But come to think of it, it was hardly known—and most certainly hadn't achieved Olympic status—when she died in 1975.

But it was Kellerman who really invented synchronised swimming back around the turn of the century, although she didn't call it that and she most certainly didn't frolic in the pool with one of those ridiculous pegs on her nose. To her it was formation swimming and she drew large crowds to venues around the world to watch her troupe of 'aqua-belles' go through their paces.

Kellerman was the first woman swimmer to grab the headlines. And she did that with monotonous regularity throughout her life, especially when pursuing her one-woman

ANNETTE KELLERMAN

campaign to allow those of her sex to wear comfortable swimming costumes.

She learned to swim at Cavill's Natatorium in Sydney, originally taking up the sport to strengthen her legs in the wake of a childhood illness (believed to have been polio). She became so proficient that, in February 1902, at the age of 15 she won two titles—the 100 yards and the one mile—at the inaugural NSW Ladies Championships, held at St George's Baths. If there had been any Australian Championships, she would undoubtedly have proved to be the best swimmer in the country. But this was the era when national sporting officials decreed that women should only swim behind closed doors away from the lustful gaze of males.

The high-spirited young Kellerman had already shocked swimming officials with her suggestion that women should be allowed to wear a one-piece costume like the men. Shock, horror! What had got into the lass?

With no provision for women at the Olympics—that was not to come until the 1912 Stockholm Games—Kellerman's father decided to map out a professional career that would see her touring the world. With this in mind she started practising the unique underwater routines that were the inspiration for synchronised swimming.

Kellerman also worked on building up her stamina because she wanted to be the first woman to attempt the marathon swim across the English Channel—something that had remained the domain of men since Capt Matthew Webb made the first successful crossing in 1875.

With this in mind she headed off to London in early 1905.

Reports of her prowess had preceded her, especially her long-distance swimming efforts. These included one swim in Melbourne's Yarra River on 2 February 1905, in which she covered the 8 kilometres from Glen Iris to the Princes Bridge in 1 hour, 48 minutes and 34 seconds.

Once in the British capital, she began to draw huge crowds

to the London Hippodrome to watch her perform a variety of routines in a specially constructed tank. These included swimming with various fish and peeling and eating a banana underwater.

There was also a mammoth turnout on the banks of the River Thames early in June when she swam the 21 kilometres from Putney to Blackhall in three hours, 54 minutes and 16 seconds.

It was her final preparation for the ultimate swim. But sadly, on 6 July, her gallant attempt to become the first woman in the world to swim the English Channel failed after she became sea-sick and began vomiting. Her worried backup crew pulled her from the water three hours into her swim.

'I'm disappointed—but it's not the end of the world,' Kellerman told journalists. 'I intend to try again.' She did on another two occasions—but these, too, ended in failure.

In 1906 she completed a 10 kilometre swim in the River Seine and won a 40 kilometre race along the Danube, before heading for the United States.

It was in North America that Kellerman was to gain her greatest notoriety. During a successful vaudeville tour, she was arrested in 1907 on a beach in Boston, Massachusetts, for wearing what the local police claimed was an indecent swimming costume. The police claimed the garment was indecent because it was one-piece and did not cover her legs.

The arrest only added to her popularity, ensuring the success of her $2000-a-week vaudeville high diving act. Film directors lined up trying to persuade her to star in their silent movies. She accepted a couple of roles, including one in *Neptune's Daughter*. Shot in 1916 it was, at the time, the costliest movie ever made. The highlight, if you'll pardon the pun, was when Kellerman plunged from a 28 metre high cliff. It was a world record high dive for a woman.

The following year a Harvard professor conducted a survey

that chose her from 10,000 others as 'The World's Most Perfect Woman'.

Hollywood fictionalised her life story in the 1952 movie musical *The Million Dollar Mermaid* starring Esther Williams, Victor Mature and Walter Pidgeon. At the time, Kellerman, in her late sixties, was still swimming regularly and proud of her slim figure which she boasted to newsmen was 'even better than Esther's'. By the way, Esther Williams starred in a 1940 remake of Kellerman's early silent effort *Neptune's Daughter*, but it was a stunt-woman who did the high diving.

Kellerman finally returned home to Australia and settled on the Gold Coast in 1970, four years before she was inducted into the International Swimming Hall of Fame in Fort Lauderdale, Florida. She died in a hospital at Southport on 6 November 1975, aged 89.

A Combo by Any Other Name

In the late nineteenth century the mecca for the finest professional runners in the world was the Sir Joseph Banks Hotel in the Sydney suburb of Botany.

The hotel was built back in 1834 on huge grounds on the foreshores of Botany Bay. It was the setting for Australia's first zoo with dozens of breeds of animals from around the world— elephants, giraffe, chimpanzee, monkeys, bears and various species of deer. Yes, and Australian marsupials, too.

But the lure of these exotic fauna was nothing compared with the appeal of the world's best sprinters, who regularly competed on the Carrington Athletic Ground adjacent to the hotel. The fans would flock to Botany to watch races such as the Sir Joseph Banks Grand Handicap. First conducted in 1879 and run over 130 yards, it was reputedly the richest event in the world.

The Botany races were also unusual. In a period where many white sportsmen refused to compete against those of coloured races, mine host at the Sir Joseph Banks Hotel, Frank Smith, actively encouraged Aborigines to compete in the events he organised. Overseas stars, many of them racially intolerant, had no alternative but to accept their presence if they wanted a chance to carry off some of the booty offered by Smith.

One of the greatest of all the Aboriginal runners was Charlie Daniels, alias Sambo Combo. He grew up on the Jimbour cattle station owned by Sir Joshua Bell about 20 kilometres north of Dalby on Queensland's Darling Downs. Speed was obviously in the family genes for his elder brother, George Combo, was already a recognised star quarter-miler on the professional circuit when William Robinson, a stockman at Jimbour, took the younger of the pair to Sydney.

Robinson wanted to beat the bookies so he changed Sambo Combo's name to Daniels. Otherwise the price would have been too short and the handicaps too tough. Daniels' first appearance in the Grand Handicap, in 1885, ended in abject failure. But Robinson knew his true worth and he took him back gain the following year.

The bookies were unimpressed. After all, Daniels was not a solid specimen—standing only 5 feet 8 inches tall and weighing just 9 stone 4 pounds. But Robinson knew of his long stride which averaged almost 7 feet 5 inches and the young sprinter's explosive power over distances up to 300 yards. And he was unconcerned that Daniels was a chain-smoker.

Off a handicap of 14 yards, Daniels won the 1886 Grand

Handicap with consummate ease, beating a well-known local, Ted Lazarus, by eight yards in the time of 13.4 seconds. For his efforts Daniels received 150 sovereigns and a gold watch.

It was the start of a brilliant, if all too short, career.

His best efforts came in the 1887–88 seasons. He was set against the English world champion Harold Hutchens in a series of match races over 150 yards in Sydney, beating him effortlessly. Daniels also accounted for Irish star Tom Malone, who had world records from 120 yards to 440 yards to his credit.

In 1888 Daniels was timed at 9.1 seconds over 100 yards— a time not equalled until 75 years later by the American Bob Hayes, who a year later won the 1964 Olympic 100m crown. Daniels also ran a 300-yard event in 30 seconds in 1888.

It was therefore no surprise when tens of thousands of spectators turned up at Botany for the eighth running of the Sir Joseph Banks Grand Handicap. They came in all forms of transport from coach and horseback to the steam-tram and had eyes only for Daniels. He did not disappoint them. Even though he didn't win, Daniels ran the 130 yards in 12.5 seconds—a record for all the Australian colonies.

It was the handicapper who had finally beaten him. And Daniels decided that he'd had enough. His final words were: 'All I want is a bridle and a saddle. I want to go home.' And so saying he headed back to the Darling Downs.

Further Back than Walla Walla

Only a few living creatures have managed to have their names immortalised in the Australian 'slanguage'. The supposed sexual prowess of Australia's Hollywood heart-throb Errol Flynn resulted in the expression 'in like Flynn'. Then there was the World War II rallying cry 'Up there Cazaly', derived from the brilliant marking of Aussie Rules great Roy Cazaly.

Over the years, racecallers have also been fond of using the expression 'he's covered more ground than Burke and Wills' (as in the explorers Robert O'Hara Burke and William John Wills, who perished in central Australia). This is a way of describing a horse going wide for most of the race and therefore ruining any chance of success.

As mentioned elsewhere in this book, the racehorse Drongo gave his name to the proverbial dill.

And finally there was Walla Walla. For more than half a century the phrase 'further back than Walla Walla' has been used on racecourses around the nation. It's a way of describing a horse in an apparently hopeless position.

It's also a contradiction in terms. For Walla Walla was a freakish horse who managed to win major harness horse races and set dozens of pacing records even though handicappers forced him to concede huge starts to his opposition.

Walla Walla was a bay horse fathered by one of the greatest sires of pacers in Australian history, Globe Derby.

Out of the mare Princess Winona, Walla Walla was foaled in 1922. Considering his later exploits, it is surprising that he never set foot on a trotting track until six years later when he won an inconsequential race at a country show at Gunning, about 80 kilometres north of Canberra.

Over the next five years, Walla Walla won races in all states except Western Australia, as well as New Zealand. His best year was undoubtedly 1933, when he was nine years old.

On 15 May that year, at Sydney's Harold Park Paceway, he set a time of 2 minutes 2.4 seconds for the mile from a rolling start, an Australasian record that was to stand for seven years. He slashed more than a second off the old mark of 2 minutes 3.6 seconds set by a New Zealand pacer, Akron. The trotting authorities had given every encouragement to Walla Walla and his owner-trainer LS Martin, who drove the champion. They were paced by two trotters and a cantering pony.

That same year, Walla Walla won an event over a mile and a half (2400 metres) at Harold Park from a handicap of 180 yards (165 metres) behind.

This wasn't the biggest handicap ever given to Walla Walla. In 1929, he had been forced to start 288 yards (263 metres) behind the rest of the field in a race at Goulburn, in the NSW southern tablelands. It proved to be too much. He finished third. But at the same track in 1934 he won the Goulburn Gold Cup over one and a half miles from a handicap of 132 yards (121 metres).

Another great effort on the track was at Addington, New Zealand, in 1934. From a standing start Walla Walla clocked 2 minutes 4.2 seconds for the mile, a then world record. At least in that appearance he didn't have to beat the handicapper as well as the timekeeper!

Double or Nothing

In his dotage, Dirk Wellham will certainly have something to tell his grandchildren. Sitting back in his rocking chair, he will be able to muse about his unique record as far as Australian cricket is concerned. And the youngsters at his feet will shake their heads and look at each other with knowing looks. 'Grandpa's at it again!'

And well he should have a bit of a boast. For Wellham did something none of the more famous Australian cricketers managed. Not 'The Don', Victor Trumper, Bill Ponsford or Archie Jackson. Nor Dougie Walters or AB. Chappelli? Perish the thought!

Wellham scored a century in his first-class debut and again in his Test debut. Yes, one other player, the Indian Gundappa Viswanath, had managed it before. But no one else in the world had done so. Certainly not an Aussie.

The young batsman from the Sydney suburb of Summer Hill had set many a record as a schoolboy. But it was when Wellham hit a ton at his first appearance for New South Wales, against Victoria during the 1980–81 season, that people really began to sit up and take notice. With only four more first-class matches under his belt he was chosen in the Australian side to tour England in 1981. At first he was overlooked for the major matches, but he finally got a break in the sixth Test, at The Oval. Wellham scored 103 to join a select few who had scored debut Test centuries.

And the unique Aussie double was his.

Of course, selectors are strange creatures. He was dropped

for the next Test, back in Australia, and never again given a real chance to consolidate. So was the double a fluke? You would have to ask the selectors!

But, by the way, it should be pointed out that there is another record to which Wellham can lay claim. He is the only man in history to have captained three Australian state sides—New South Wales, Tasmania and Queensland—in the Sheffield Shield.

And that was certainly no fluke!

Give Me a Break

In the so-called good old days, major billiards tournaments attracted big crowds. Of course there were plenty of side bets among the patrons, all away from the prying eyes of the constabulary. But it was good, clean entertainment.

Then along came Walter Lindrum. And, with his freakish play, he single-handedly killed off billiards as a spectator sport. He was so supreme that they virtually scrapped the world championships until he retired. No one would play him unless he offered mammoth starts. And it was no use having a side bet—Lindrum always won. Even changing the rules failed to curb his talents.

By the time of his death in 1960 few tournaments were staged and it was left to the sister sport of snooker to grab the public's interest.

That is Walter Lindrum's legacy!

He was born (on 29 August 1898) into a family with the love of billiards coursing through their veins. His father, Fred Lindrum, was a publican in the rip-roaring goldfields city of

WALTER LINDRUM
—he showed promise as a teenager.

Kalgoorlie. Fred was proud to be a Sandgroper and it is said that is why he had his son baptised Walter Albert Lindrum, so he would have the state's initials in his name. Or so the story goes, and who are we to say it isn't true?

Fred Lindrum won the Native-Born Championship of Australia at Melbourne in 1887 (a tournament designed to stop visiting Englishmen from claiming the Australian crown). He had also earlier beaten the English champion John Roberts Jnr, when the Englishman toured Australia in 1876. Fred was determined his children would succeed in his chosen sport, too. And he was a hard taskmaster, demanding they practice at the billiards table from an early age for at least eight hours a day. It paid off. His eldest son, Fred Jnr became Australian professional champion as a teenager and toured the country in 1907 with the English star Melbourne Inman (who was to have the title of world champion bestowed upon him the following year, even though there was no tournament to decide the crown). Fred Jnr then tried his luck in England, where at the age of 20 he was feted by another group as the unofficial world champion.

The British regarded him as the finest player Australia had ever produced. At least they did until Walter arrived on the scene.

To complete the family connection, their sister Violet won the Australian women's championship and later their nephew Horace Lindrum became world snooker champion (in 1952) and achieved the maximum possible break of 147 in an exhibition at Penrith, west of Sydney, in 1941.

When he was three, Walter Lindrum suffered an accident in which his right index finger was crushed. As a result, he taught himself to play billiards left-handed. He chalked up his first century break at the age of 12 at Belfield's Hotel in Sydney and his first 500 at 14. But he remained in Fred Jnr's shadow and his eldest brother went on the record in 1921 as saying Walter was not of championship ability because he had never beaten him in an official tournament. Not for long!

Walter Lindrum achieved international recognition the following year when he made a world-record break of 1417 in a match against English star and former world champion Harry Stevenson, who was visiting Australia.

Lindrum eventually ran out of competition in Australia and, in 1930, headed for England. The British authorities used a technicality to prevent him from taking part in the World Professional Championships. But he proved his worth by making 67 breaks of 1000 or more during his stay, including a then personal best of 3262.

In a match against Willie Smith, world champion in 1920 and 1923, he made 11 breaks of over 1000. At Manchester, Lindrum made a break of 1011 in less than half an hour. He also won the Empire Tournament in London beating yet another former world champion, Tom Newman, by 1371 in the final.

The following season Lindrum was back in Britain again.

By that time Lindrum had set a world record break of 3905 and he'd made a vow to break it in the Old Dart. The stories say that before leaving Australia he had accepted a bet at 3 to 1 that he couldn't top the mark and another at 2 to 1 that he couldn't make a break of more than 4000.

If that is true, on Wednesday, 30 January 1932, he won both bets. It was at Thurston Hall in London, the most famous billiards venue in the world. His opponent was the reigning world champion Joe Davis, who had held the world crown since 1928. The previous day Lindrum had made an unfinished break of 3151. When he resumed he appeared nervous and almost missed several shots that normally would have been quite simple. But he soon got into a rhythm.

When he reached 3905 he calmly paused to chalk his cue. Then, when he broke the record, he paused to acknowledge a standing ovation from the crowd, making a brief speech of thanks. He continued on relentlessly. During the evening session he finally made a mistake, missing a difficult nursery cannon after leaving one of the balls a centimetre off line. The record break was finally over at 4137. His record effort had taken just under three hours—171 minutes to be exact. The mammoth break had included 1295 nursery cannons—Lindrum's favourite way of racking up big scores.

Of the day's play, Lindrum said: 'I felt a little uncomfortable in the first 10 minutes. Resuming from overnight is not good. But when I warmed up I felt confident. And when I reached 4000 I thought I could go on indefinitely. It was just a little kick of my ball that brought the position that crashed me.'

Davis, thoroughly beaten despite Lindrum giving him a big start, said: 'This feat is truly astounding. It was a wonderful example of dual control. Control of the brain and of the billiard balls.'

The Times newspaper reported the event in glowing terms: 'Lindrum's feat is remarkable. He is not only supreme in scoring but he plays with unequalled ease and rapidity. Since he first came here he has constantly set himself a higher mark. At the same time the excellence of his play seems to have improved that of his fellow professionals.'

On that visit to England there was also the added bonus of an invitation from King George V to visit Buckingham Palace. In the Royal Billiard Room, His Majesty asked Lindrum to show him a few of his shots. The Australian demonstrated no fewer than 150 different shots. When he had finished, King George said: 'I must congratulate you. That is really wonderful.' And he duly presented Lindrum with a pair of gold cufflinks inscribed with the royal crest. The champion was to wear the cufflinks at every public appearance until his retirement from the sport some two decades later.

Lindrum's domination of the sport—even though he was still not allowed to compete for the world title—forced the authorities to change the rules in an attempt to curb his mammoth breaks. A limit of 25 was placed on the number of successive nursery cannons any player could make.

But it did not stop Lindrum. He was still unbeatable. Finally, in 1933 he got his chance to play in the World Professional Championships. As expected, he won, although Newman held him to a margin of 1218 in their semi-final and Davis to 694 in the final.

In a real breakthrough the English Billiards Association, the ruling world body, allowed Lindrum to defend his crown in Australia the following year, but only if he would share the profits with his two challengers, Davis and New Zealander Clark McConachy, who had fought out the 1932 final. Once again Lindrum emerged triumphant, beating Davis in the final by 875. He was to remain world champion until his retirement in 1950. Only then did McConachy get his chance to take the crown and, by that time, he was 56 years old.

There were further rule changes, this time concerning the baulk-line. But Lindrum always remained supreme, setting a new world record break under these rules of 1796 at David Jones' store in Sydney on 3 June 1936.

Some of his other great efforts over the years included a 663 break in 15 minutes (in London in 1930), 346 breaks in eight minutes (in Melbourne in 1932 and again in 1952), reaching 100 in 46 seconds (in Sydney in 1941) and breaks of 3737 and 3752 in consecutive visits to the table (in Melbourne in 1944).

Lindrum was awarded the MBE in 1951 and the OBE in 1958. Over the years it is estimated he raised more than $6 million for various charities and World War II patriotic funds with exhibitions around Australia. He died after a heart attack in Surfers Paradise on the Queensland Gold Coast on 30 July 1960, aged 61. Admirers raised money for an elaborate gravestone in the Melbourne cemetery where he was buried—a green marble full-sized billiards table, complete with white marble pockets and three bronze billiard balls and a cue on top.

It Was Hardly Cricket

George Coulthard was an outstanding Aussie Rules player with Carlton in the 1870s and a renowned umpire. He is said to have been the first to wear the distinctive white coat to distinguish himself from the players, at a time when the two captains used to also act as umpires.

He was also a better-than-average cricketer and one of only two men to have umpired a Test before actually playing in one. He umpired the only Test of the 1878–79 season when Lord Harris brought his team to Australia. And he made his lone appearance in the Test arena as a player in the second Test of the 1881–82 series, at the Sydney Cricket Ground. In his only innings he batted number 11, remaining six not out, and did not get to bowl.

This most certainly had something to do with the fact that Billy Murdoch was Australian captain and he had previously been at the centre of an infamous incident for which he blamed Coulthard. Sadly, it is for this incident that Coulthard is best remembered in the annals of cricket.

It was on Saturday, 8 February 1879, the second day of the match between Lord Harris' English side and New South Wales. The day that 2000 spectators at the Sydney Cricket Ground staged the worst riot in Australian cricket history.

Lord Harris had brought the 22-year-old Coulthard from Melbourne to be his umpire in three matches in New South Wales. The other umpire at the SCG was Edmund Barton, later to become Australia's first Prime Minister.

Murdoch, who had starred in an earlier encounter with the

Englishmen, was a favourite with the crowd, especially those who had bet heavily on New South Wales despite police warnings that anyone caught gambling at the Sydney Cricket Ground faced a jail sentence.

The English side led by 90 runs on the first innings and forced the home side to follow on. Murdoch began fluently until he reached 10. It was then that he went for a quick single and was run out. It was Coulthard who raised his right index finger.

The spectators were livid. They jumped the fence and headed for Coulthard and the Englishmen. It was reported that Lord Harris was hit across the back with a whip and someone else whacked Coulthard with a stick.

Albert 'Monkey' Hornby, a tough sportsman who also represented England in rugby, went to Lord Harris' aid and had the shirt ripped off his back. He wrestled with the culprit and carried him to the pavilion with the angry mob in hot pursuit. There he handed the miscreant over to police.

It was said that two of the Englishmen, Tom Emmett and George 'Happy Jack' Ulyett, inflamed the situation by calling the demonstrators 'sons of convicts'. It took half an hour to clear the offenders from the field and even longer for NSW captain Dave Gregory to be placated. The match eventually resumed on the following Monday.

Several of the rioters ended up in court, where they were fined £2 with £1/5/- court costs.

An angry Lord Harris described them in reports back to London newspapers as 'a howling mob'. But Test cricketer Tom Horan was not impressed with His Lordship. Writing in the *Australasian* under the pen name Felix, Horan noted: 'Lord Harris owns to a sly kick or two ... Victorian cricketers have experienced rougher treatment more than once on Sydney fields, but they took it like men.'

The riot cost Sydney a Test match, with Lord Harris

taking his side back to Melbourne for another game against Victoria instead.

It was Coulthard's one moment of notoriety. On 22 October 1883 he died from tuberculosis. He was just 27 years old.

Last Ditch Effort

Hal Hooker was a member of the Light Horse Cavalry during World War I. He was one of those heroes depicted by legendary Australian movie director Charles Chauvel in his classic 1940 epic *Forty Thousand Horsemen*, the story of the greatest cavalry charge of the twentieth century, at Beersheba in Palestine.

But this is a story of a different type of brave stand. It is the story of one of the most remarkable efforts in the history of first-class cricket, one that still has cricket enthusiasts shaking their heads in disbelief some 70 years later.

Hooker was what is commonly known in cricket circles as a 'rabbit'. As a batsman he made a good bowler. Indeed, during the eight seasons he had in first-class cricket his efforts in wielding the willow netted him a meagre 421 runs. His average of 20 was helped along by the fact that he inevitably came in last and in almost one-third of his 30 appearances at the crease he had come away with his wicket intact. His partners at the other end would get themselves out trying to score quick, last-minute runs.

Then came that remarkable single innings that sealed his place in history.

It began on Christmas Day, 1928. Victoria was in the box

seat in the Sheffield Shield clash at the Melbourne Cricket Ground. They had rattled up a first innings score of 376 and soon had the star-studded NSW line-up reeling at 8 for 74. Of the recognised batsmen Archie Jackson had managed just 19, Tommy Andrews 33 and Don Bradman just a single. There was a brief rally, but when Hooker strode to the crease to join Alan Kippax it was 9 for 113.

All seemed lost. But Hooker was determined to stay around to give Kippax some much-needed batting practice on the Melbourne wicket.

'The Sheffield Shield match had been scheduled for Christmas Day because the Ashes Test would be played over New Year,' Hooker was to recall later. 'Alan was in the Test side, but he had never done well in Melbourne. All he wanted to do was get some time in the middle.'

And that's exactly what he did!

The Victorian captain Jack Ryder had his fieldsmen clustered around the rabbit Hooker trying to unnerve him. But it was all in vain. Hooker was a picture of concentration and at one stage called out to Ryder, waving his bat at the close-in fieldsmen: 'Hey Jack, could you pull a couple of these blokes back a bit? I'd like to be able to see the bowler coming in, if you don't mind!'

Hooker was also suffering physically, unable to relieve himself during breaks.

But he stuck around.

'After a while I thought, well I'd better hold up my end to give Alan a chance to get his century,' And Kippax did. 'Then he came to me and noted we only needed 150 to pass the Victorians. So, I kept my bat straight and we headed for that target.' By the end of the day, the New South Welshmen were only nine runs in arrears.

By this time, Kippax had posted a double-century and Hooker a half-century. Hooker had driven his first boundary of the innings to bring up the 200 partnership. And he had grabbed his half-century with two full-blooded fours of successive balls from Hunter 'Stork' Hendry.

Overnight, Hooker was in such pain, unable to empty his bladder, that he was rushed to hospital. But he was back the next day to continue his fight.

The pair duly knocked off the 10 runs needed to overtake the Victorians and continued to thwart the bowlers' efforts until the score reached 420. It was only then that Hooker made a poor stroke and Ryder snapped up a catch in slips off the bowling of Ted a'Beckett. Hooker was out for 62. But the New South Wales pair had posted a world record last-wicket partnership of 307, scored in only 304 minutes.

'I tried to hit a'Beckett out of the ground,' Hooker explained. 'Kippax was furious and, as we walked off the field, he made it clear just how angry he was.'

'I had been riding you for a century and you had to go and mess it up,' he fumed at Hooker.

Hooker, too, was angry. A couple of years before his death in 1982 at the age of 83, he explained: 'I hadn't missed a ball in two days and I went and did a stupid thing like that. More than 50 years later I still regret the rush of blood to my head. It's enough to make you cry. People say it was a fluke. But I never batted better in my life.'

The match was to peter out to a draw. But none of the crowd of 10,000 that had witnessed the partnership on each day really minded. They had been there when history was made.

Oh, yes. And that batting practice that Kippax got during the world record partnership certainly paid dividends. In the Test against England, a week later, he scored 100 in Australia's first innings and 41 in the second.

As for Hooker, well it proved to be a good season for him. In the return match against Victoria, at the Sydney Cricket Ground, he ended the visitors' first innings with a hat-trick. And then with his first ball in the second innings he also snared a wicket. With this he became the first bowler to take four wickets in four balls in Australian first-class cricket.

A Case of Mistaken Identity

Tasmanian batsman Kenny Burn should never have got the chance to play cricket for Australia. His selection was purely a case of mistaken identity. And as such it has become part of cricketing legend.

Not that he was a duffer. Indeed, Kenny Burn was a more than competent cricketer. As a virtually unknown 25-year-old he had hit 99 not out for Tasmania against the 1887–88 English side captained by Middlesex's George Vernon (one of two English teams to tour Australia that season).

When selectors Harry Boyle and Jack Blackman sat down to choose an Australian side to tour England in 1890, they needed a second wicket-keeper to give Blackham a chance of a rest when minor matches were scheduled. They had read of the exploits of the Tasmanian named Burn and sent an invitation to Kenny Burn to join them in the squad.

It was only when he arrived to join the ship in Adelaide that they realised their blunder. They had chosen the wrong Burn. The Tasmanian mentioned in despatches was John Burn. Kenny Burn explained that he had never kept wickets in his life. But they decided he should tour anyway. It was said that such was Burn's lack of worldliness that he arrived in Adelaide at the start of the tour with just a tiny suitcase containing one change of clothes and a bag of toiletries.

As it subsequently turned out, during the tour every player except Burn had at least one spell as wicket-keeper. But he did play as a batsman in both Tests, at Lord's and The Oval. He was all at sea on the soft English wickets, with a duck and 19 in the first Test and 7 and 15 in the second encounter. The two matches were won by England.

Burn was never given another chance in the Test arena. But his record shows that he represented Tasmania from 1883 to 1910, captaining the colony-cum-state for 20 years. During the 1907–08 season, then aged 45, Burn hit a century against Arthur Jones' touring English side. In Hobart grade cricket he posted top scores of 365 and 361.

Kenny Burn died in the Tasmanian capital in 1956. At 93 he had been the oldest living Test cricketer.

The Judge Couldn't Split Them

There is only one recorded instance in the history of horse racing where four horses dead-heated for first in a race. Of course, it was in the dim, distant past before the invention of the photo finish. It was a fluke finish back then. It would be even more of a fluke today.

The unique end to the race took place at the southern Queensland town of Toowoomba. On 2 June 1896, in the Shorts Handicap over six furlongs (1200 metres) four flashed across the line as one—Minster Belle, Lord Rosebery, Blucher and Cornet.

In those days the prizemoney wasn't split except with the

owners' agreement. So the poor nags had to go out and complete the course a second time. Cornet won the run-off.

But occasionally run-offs weren't decisive. There are several instances of horses dead-heating twice.

At the Northern Jockey Club's meeting at Armidale on 12 August 1896, three horses—Syndicate, Tom and Yellow Plush—dead-heated for first in the Flying Handicap over six furlongs (1200 metres). In the run-off Tom and Yellow Plush dead-heated once again. They tried a third time and this time the weary Tom managed to get up to win ... by a half-head.

The pair could not have been as weary as The Flying Dutchman and Saladin who dead-heated in the 1872 Australian Cup over two and a quarter miles (3.6 kilometres) at the Melbourne track of Flemington. They raced off over the marathon journey a second time. And once again the judge couldn't separate them. At the third attempt Saladin got up to win the big race.

At the Moorefield track in Sydney on 17 October 1903, three horses—Loch Lochie, High Flier and Barinda—finished in a dead-heat for first in the Moorefield Handicap over one and a quarter miles (2000 metres). The run-off resulted in a second dead-heat between the three horses. It was then that the owners got together and decided to split the prizemoney.

But what about Sir Ross and Bay Hart? They dead-heated three times at Rockhampton on 9 September 1922, before the owners split the purse. It is believed to be the only instance of this happening anywhere in the world.

Wocko Was Wide of the Mark

There have been many strange sporting selections over the years. One can only wonder what got into the minds of the selectors as they chose the name of this unknown and that non-performer. Did they throw all the names in a hat and randomly pick one out? Had they partaken of too much singing syrup before sitting down for their deliberations? Needless to say, we will never know.

To this day cricket fans wonder about the 1973 Test selection of 'Wocko'—as spinner John Watkins was known around the coalfields of the Hunter Valley. He'd played a few seasons of grade cricket in Sydney. But, at the time he was drafted into the Test side for the third Test against the touring Pakistanis, he had played only five first-class matches for New South Wales in which he had taken just 10 wickets at a less-than-flattering average of 36.90.

But a few weeks earlier he had taken 6 for 38 when Northern New South Wales scored a surprise win over the tourists in a non-first-class match. This obviously influenced the Test selectors when they made what to all critics was a baffling selection.

The Test proved to be a huge embarrassment for Watkins, despite him scoring 36 in a record ninth wicket partnership of 83 with paceman Bob Massie. After all, Wocko wasn't in the side for his batting.

His nervous bowling effort was a disaster, with six overs

of full tosses, long hops and balls almost too wide for the batsmen to reach. Eventually Australia's captain Ian Chappell had no option other than to take him off.

The story is told that after the match was over and Wocko was back in his home city, one hurtful fellow in Newcastle's Cricketers' Arms Hotel approached him and explained: 'You'd have bowled great if it had been a month earlier when the Sheffield Shield match was in progress. You kept landing the ball on the Shield pitch. It's just a pity you were playing the Test on the pitch adjacent to it!'

As a postscript, Watkins was taken to the West Indies on the subsequent tour. The nervousness remained and he played only four matches. It is perhaps significant that he then completed his cricket career in Newcastle grade cricket ... as a batsman.

King of the Ring

In the 1950s, the Baby Boomers would flock to the Saturday arvo flicks to watch Hopalong Cassidy, the Lone Ranger and Tonto and the 'King of the Cowboys' Roy Rogers. Well, not quite. The Baby Boomers' parents used to extol the virtues of Roy and his trusty steed Trigger. But, if truth be known, Roy was passé by the 1950s.

Come to think of it there were more than a few Hollywood cowboys who were passé. Blokes like Gabby Hayes never quite made it to the superstardom that would hold our attention before it became time to roll our Jaffas down the aisle of the local theatre.

And what about Tom Mix?

SNOWY BAKER

He wasn't a bad sort of a cowboy, although we read about him in comics rather than watched him on the silver screen. But while researching for this tome, I discovered that he did appear in a few movies. There was *My Pal*, the celluloid offering of 1932. It was a surefire winner at the box office because not only was Tom Mix riding across the screen but it also starred Mickey Rooney. According to the plot, Tom Mix taught Mickey the ways of the Wild West.

Well, he may have done so up there on the flickering screen. But if we are to believe the stories about Aussie sportsman 'Snowy' Baker, Tom Mix didn't even know how to ride a horse until the bloke from Sydney taught him how. And while we're on the subject ... why not add Rudolf Valentino in the 1921 potboiler *The Sheik*, the story about the English woman abducted by an Arab for a bit of slap and tickle in the desert that made Valentino the star that women swooned over. Baker taught him how to ride and while galloping at full speed snatch wenches from the ground and throw them over the back of his horse.

Baker is credited with teaching Douglas Fairbanks (that's senior, not junior) how to crack a whip for his 1925 role in *Don Q, Son of Zorro*. The whip came in handy as Fairbanks rescued Mary Astor from a fate worse than death (at least that's the way the studio described it).

And remember *National Velvet* and the innocent youth of Elizabeth Taylor? Baker was supposed to have tutored her, too, in the finer arts of riding a galloper to victory in the Grand National.

Whether or not any or all of these happened, Baker told everyone they did after his one return home from Hollywood in 1952. He was to die, aged 69, on 2 December the following year.

What is not in dispute was that Snowy Baker established a record for himself as possibly the greatest all-round sportsman Australia has ever known before he headed off for the good ol' US of A in 1920. He excelled in a host of different sports—some historians suggest as many as 26.

At 11 he was Sydney All Schools' athletic champion. Two years later he was a New South Wales open-age swimming champion. He made his first-grade rugby union debut with Eastern Suburbs at 15 and as a 20-year-old played two Tests against the touring 1904 British Lions. He also won rowing, fencing, diving, polo and wrestling titles. At Sydney University where he studied engineering he was awarded 'blues' in athletics, cricket, rowing and rugby union.

But it was as a boxer that Baker was best. He was an Australian amateur champion in 1905 and 1906 and after the latter success headed off for England to take on the finest the British could offer.

He was laid low by a bout of typhoid fever and was still in Britain when it came time for the 1908 Olympics, for which he had accepted an invitation to represent Australia. His first efforts were in the pool, finishing sixth in the springboard diving and fourth as a member of the $4 \times 200m$ freestyle swimming side (with six-time Olympic medallist Frank Beaurepaire, Frank Springfield and Theo Tartakover).

Later in the Olympics, Baker lost a controversial fight in the final of the middleweight division boxing. He had beaten three British opponents (two by knockout) on the one day en route to the gold medal showdown later that evening. Baker's opponent in the final was JWHT Douglas, who was later to make a name for himself as England's cricket captain. The famous Australian barracker, Yabba, upset about his characteristic slow batting, dubbed him 'Johnny Won't Hit Today' Douglas.

Well, he did hit out in the Olympic encounter with Baker. It was a torrid battle. One of the ringside judges gave the fight to Baker, the other to Douglas. The deciding vote in Douglas' favour came from the referee—who just happened to be Douglas' father. To be fair, Baker always claimed it was a fair result. Soon after the Games, the pair met again in a bare-knuckle bout at London's National Sporting Club, a bout that finished with Baker knocking out his Olympic conqueror.

No Australian has ever done better in the Olympic boxing ring. Only Grahame 'Spike' Cheney has matched Baker's effort, with a silver medal at the 1988 Seoul Olympics.

Baker spent a couple of years touring Britain and Europe, giving sporting exhibitions and taking on all comers in boxing and wrestling bouts. Returning home to Sydney he opened a gym and began publishing *Snowy Baker's Magazine*, devoted to physical fitness sports with more than a few scurrilous editorials when the Olympian had a personal axe to grind.

In 1913 Baker bought the Sydney Stadium off Hugh D McIntosh (known around the traps as 'Huge Deal'). On 3 October that year Baker convened a conference of boxing managers, trainers and promoters, who for the first time in Australia agreed upon a standard set of weights and conditions for championship fights. Of course, Baker promoted most of the major ones through his company Stadiums Ltd, which he sold to the notorious John Wren two years later.

It was then that Baker decided on a movie career. Australia was at the forefront of this burgeoning industry and Snowy was clever enough to understand its potential. He became an Australian super-hero, fighting the forces of evil and winning the coy maidens' hearts. The profits from his acting career he turned back into film-making. He bought a huge mansion in the eastern suburbs of Sydney and converted it into some of the most modern studios in the world. He lured a few of the most promising American directors to Sydney to make his movies.

Most of these efforts have been lost in the dimness of time but they are said to have included *The Man from Kangaroo*, about a boxing priest, and *The Shadow of Lightning Ridge*, the story of a handsome bushranger, totally misunderstood by the constabulary.

SNOWY BAKER
Teaching yet another Hollywood starlet

It was only natural that Baker's career would eventually find him in Hollywood. But once there, he remained largely on the periphery, investing in the Riviera Country Club at Santa Monica, where the well-to-do Hollywood figures would gather to play polo. Baker is said to have met the silent movie comedian Harold Lloyd at the club and the pair became firm friends for life.

Again, it's hard to tell fact from fiction, for Baker was the ultimate self-propagandist. All we *can* say is he was a damned good sportsman. A sporting freak!

The Ultimate Cricket Groupie

Cricket fans are like no others. The Carlton supporter may make a trip every year to Sydney to watch the Blues take on the Swans. Tennis freaks may make the once in a life-time pilgrimage to Wimbledon. And rugby league supporters ... well they used to join the tours organised by the doyen of Sydney broadcasters Frank Hyde, but that had a lot to do with Frank's bonhomie and the way he would organise singalongs with him grating out his famous rendition of 'Oh Danny Boy'.

But cricket fanatics are a breed apart. They will buy every last book published—even when there are too many published and the resultant spending means that the kids miss out on the annual trip to the *Ekka* or the Royal Easter Show.

And they travel the world on supporters' tours. Indeed, they'll go every year if there is enough of the folding stuff. A cricket fan's life is incomplete without at least one appearance at Lord's, Basin Reserve, Wanderers, Eden Gardens, Gaddafi Stadium and Sabina Park.

The rain at Lord's, the anticipation of a possible crowd riot at Eden Gardens and the distinctive aroma of exotic cheroots at Sabina Park only enhances the appeal of these famous cricket arenas. To cricket fans, these places are holy shrines as are Mecca to the Muslims and Jerusalem to the Christians and Jews.

Joy is just sitting in the stand at Headingley, Leeds. On one side it faces the rugby league ground, where the fine Aussies Vic Hey, Arthur Clues and Eric Harris (dubbed 'The Toowoomba Ghost') once held sway. On the other it looks over the cricket pitch where in 1934 Don Bradman hit a majestic 334 and four years later followed it up with 304. Bliss!

Or maybe the pressure cooker that is Chidambaran Stadium in Madras—or whatever they call the city now—where in 1986 a dehydrated Dean Jones scored 210 and Greg Matthews snared a leg-before-wicket decision with the last ball to force a tie. You feel the heat even when the stadium is empty.

Yes, cricket fans will go anywhere to watch their game!

But if there was ever to be an award for the greatest cricket 'groupie' in history is would surely go to Dr Rowley Pope. For four or five decades the good doctor followed Australian Test sides—and some Australian sides which weren't of Test status—around the world. Paying his own way and helping out in the true blue amateur tradition.

It should be pointed out that Dr Pope was a fair sort of a cricketer himself.

Contemporary reports say he learned his cricket while at Hutchins School in Hobart from Tom Kendall, one of Australia's heroes in the first Test match ever played, in March 1877. The left-arm bowler spun his way through the English batting line-up in their second innings, grabbing seven wickets for 55 runs and giving Australia a 45-run victory in that historic encounter.

Kendall went with the Aussie team to England the following year but his visit was aborted mid-tour—sent home because his love of strong drink caused a few embarrassing incidents. But he did prove to be a good coach.

At the end of 1884 Pope made his debut for New South Wales and, when the top players refused the money offered to play against the touring English side in the January Test in Melbourne, he made his one and only Test appearance. Sadly it was hardly a triumph for Kendall's coaching. As the cliché says, Pope didn't worry the scorers in the first innings. He followed up the duck with just three runs in the second. It was his first and last Test.

But cricket was in his blood and he began accompanying sides around the world as unpaid medical officer, baggage man and, sometimes, scorer. He didn't travel light. Perish the thought. Forty pieces of luggage were the norm. In them he had every conceivable thing that a cricketer would need—and many that he wouldn't.

Splints, bandages, sleeping pills, tablets to ease seasickness, sunburn cream, scissors, shoelaces, creams to ease haemorrhoids, scalpels, ear plugs, assorted spectacles in case players broke their glasses, toilet paper, soap, liniment ... and, of course, day-to-day things like pens, bottles of ink and notepaper.

On the 1899 tour of England, he also carried a buttonhook used to help the great all-rounder Monty Noble fasten his boots which didn't have laces. Pope got his reward by playing in a few minor matches on the 1886 tour and against Cambridge University in 1902.

And he was an expert on social etiquette—even teaching some of the lesser-educated players rudimentary skills such as how to tie a bow tie.

Captains loved him. He would always have a trunk full of

books on the areas that the team would visit. And the skippers would search him out when preparing their speeches to the local dignitaries.

Such was the case in the unofficial tour of North America in 1932—organised by the great spin bowler and cartoonist Arthur Mailey. The skipper was Victor Richardson who asked for Pope's help when he discovered the good doctor had books on everything from the American Revolution to the history of cricket in both the United States and Canada.

Pope's meticulous efforts as scorer on that tour now reveal to us that in matches at exotic places such as Moose Jaw, Kicking Horse Flats and Medicine Hat, the Aussies scored more than 10,000 runs while dismissing over 1000 batsmen. Many had been given a second chance because Mailey had decreed that no opponent should get a duck unless dismissed twice.

Pope's notes tell of matches like that against C Aubrey Smith's Hollywood XI, which included Boris Karloff. It was watched by a celebrity crowd that starred Jean Harlow and Douglas Fairbanks Jnr. Don Bradman scored 18 centuries on the tour including the team's top score of 260, against Western Ontario.

While he may have been a cricket groupie, the game owes a real debt of gratitude to the eccentric Dr Pope. On the 1938 tour of England, Bradman threatened to quit Test cricket after he was told by the authorities back in Australia that his wife Jessie would not be allowed to join him for the voyage home. Pope talked him out of such a dramatic gesture. He suggested he think about it when he had calmed down a little. And by then, the cricket chiefs back home had changed their mind.

Had Bradman cabled his letter of resignation, as he had originally intended, the cricket world would never have experienced the great tour of England by the Bradman side in 1948—some say the finest touring team in history.

Big Frank—The Boxing Kangaroo

There are plenty of yarns from the rich vein of Australian folklore that are difficult to either prove or disprove. Such is the Australian psyche that tales become, how shall we say, *enriched* when passed on from generation to generation.

You know the yarns I'm talking about. Like the one concerning media magnate Frank Packer sacking a messenger boy who, for a lark, punched the button for every floor in Packer's personal lift at his Sydney headquarters.

'How much do you earn a week, son?' growled the great man (and if you had ever met Frank Packer you would realise his presence demanded immediate response).

'Three quid,' came the reply.

'Well, here's six pounds—two weeks' salary—and you're fired.'

The kid, who had been delivering a telegram and had nothing to do with Packer's organisation, was delighted.

And what about the French crew in the America's Cup challenge in Fremantle who allegedly hit a kangaroo while driving on a sight-seeing tour somewhere on the Nullarbor? They dressed the stunned roo in the blazer owned by the team patron, the Aga Khan, and posed for photos. Suddenly the roo regained consciousness and was last seen bounding into the desert wearing the Aga Khan's blazer.

True story?

While on the subject of kangaroos, let me tell you the story about flamboyant American boxing promoter Tex Rickard and Frank the Boxing Kangaroo. The story achieved a certain respectability when published by the sports historian George Crawford in one of the thousands of illustrated newspaper columns he called *Sportifacts*. Now George has since gone to that great sporting arena in the sky, so there is no knowing where he stumbled upon the yarn. But it's worth repeating for the edification of those who enjoy a sporting tale.

Tex Rickard is best known to Australians as having allegedly (there's that word again) been involved during the 1890s and the early years of the twentieth century in the careers of our boxers Young Griffo and Les Darcy. Rickard also staged several world heavyweight title fights including the first with a million-dollar gate (between Jack Dempsey and Georges Carpentier, in 1921).

According to the Aussie yarn, in 1893 Rickard shipped a kangaroo called Big Frank from Sydney to the United States for a series of exhibition bouts. As farcical as it may seem, Big Frank apparently drew large crowds, who would roar their approval as he disposed of boxers eager for their 15 minutes of fame.

Big Frank is even said to have fought at the famous Madison Square Garden in New York, where he knocked out American heavyweight Tom Tully in the third round of their bout.

Of course, it would be crass to point out that in the 1890s Madison Square Garden, in its pre-boxing era, was home to Barnum and Bailey's circus, dubbed the *Greatest Show on Earth*. And, in 1893 Rickard was a 22-year-old gold prospector yet to be involved in boxing, or any entrepreneurial activities for that matter.

But it's a good yarn, isn't it?

'The Flying Pieman'

William Francis King was a remittance man. There were a lot of them back in the early days of the colony of New South Wales. Well-to-do Englishmen, embarrassed by the antics of their sons, would ship them off to Sydney and regularly *remit* money to keep them from coming back to the Mother Country.

King was the son of Francis King, a paymaster in the British Treasury. King Jnr arrived in the colony as a 22-year-old in 1829. And it was immediately apparent why he had been despatched Down Under. His eccentricities soon became the talk of the colony as he vainly tried his hand at schoolteaching before working as a barman in the Hope and Anchor Hotel in the centre of Sydney.

In the 1840s King became renowned for bizarre sporting feats that he performed for bets. One of the first was a marathon walking effort in which he covered more than 1600 miles (2560 kilometres) in 39 days.

He is said to have carried a dog weighing 70 pounds (32 kilograms) from Campbelltown to Sydney, a distance of 33 miles (53 kilometres), in fewer than nine hours. There are two varying reports of one other feat at Maitland Racecourse, west of Newcastle. The first story had King walking 102 miles (163 kilometres) non-stop in 24 hours. In the other version the distance was 195 miles (315 kilometres) in 46 hours, 30 minutes.

In yet another exhibition at Maitland he walked 1000 quarter-miles (400 kilometres) in 1000 quarter-hours (10 days, 10 hours). On the penultimate day King was flagging and ordered his trainer to use a horse-whip on him to keep his mind on the task ahead.

King was also a champion at running backwards. Another favourite feat was to run a mile, walk a mile, push a wheelbarrow for half-a-mile, pick up 50 stones a yard apart and make 50 standing long jumps within an hour. And he regularly took on mail coaches, beating them on the journey from Sydney to Windsor and from Brisbane to Ipswich.

When he quit athletics, he became a figure of ridicule on the streets of Sydney, selling pies in the streets of the colony while dressed in a top hat bedecked with ribbons. His customers not only got their pies but also rambling dissertations on the feats of the man who became condescendingly known as 'The Flying Pieman'.

Eventually King was committed to the Liverpool Asylum where he died of paralysis on 10 August 1873. He was given a pauper's funeral and buried in the nearby Catholic Cemetery.

Row, Row, Row Your Boat ...

Sport has thrown up many legendary figures, whose freakish ability put them head and shoulders above their contemporaries. Cricket's Don Bradman, swimming's Dawn Fraser, billiard whiz Walter Lindrum, squash player supreme Heather Mackay and the grand galloper Phar Lap are a few that spring to mind. But none emerged with the perfect record of sculler Henry Robert 'Bobby' Pearce.

Pearce was unquestionably the greatest rower the world has ever known. He was never beaten as either amateur or in the professional ranks during a career that lasted two decades. When he retired soon after World War II he did so because, quite frankly, he had run out of opponents. His superiority sounded the death-knell of the sport's popularity. Crowds of 30,000 to 50,000 watched it in the years between the two wars. But when the results became a foregone conclusion, the fans stayed at home.

Bobby Pearce was born to be a rower. It was in his genes. He came from a family of great oarsmen that lived in the waterfront suburb of Double Bay and perfected their sport on the waters of Sydney Harbour.

His grandfather, baptised Harry but known to all and sundry as 'Footy' because of his huge feet (a family trait), had emigrated from England in the late nineteenth century. Once in Sydney he soon established a name for himself as a rower. 'Footy' had the distinction of once beating the world champion sculler William Beach, one of the rare defeats suffered by the renowned Australian oarsman.

Bobby Pearce's father, Harry Jnr, twice in the years before World War I challenged unsuccessfully for the world professional title. One of Bobby's younger brothers, Sid 'Sandy' Pearce, was a very useful rower. But he made his name on the rugby league field as one of the world's greatest hookers. Fans dubbed him 'The Gentle Giant' and he played 14 Tests for Australia before a broken leg brought about a premature end to his career. And Bobby's nephew, Cecil Pearce, was three times Australian champion and represented Australia at the 1936 Berlin Olympics.

Bobby Pearce was tutored by his father to win his first race (an under-16 handicap event) when only six years old and his first open race when he was 14. It was a preview of what was to come.

Pearce won his first major title in 1927 when he took out the first of three straight Australian Amateur Championships. Unfortunately, his successes spawned a great deal of jealousy. It was an early example of Australia's infamous Tall Poppy Syndrome. Build up your champions and then cut them down to size. Only Bobby Pearce was not about to be cut down.

Everything blew up when he was chosen to compete at the 1928 Amsterdam Olympics. He was accused of having rowed professionally before his first Australian title success. The Olympic chiefs told him he couldn't go to Holland. But his accusers were left with egg on their faces. It wasn't Bobby, but one of his brothers who had competed professionally. And after he signed a statutory declaration to that effect he was back in the team.

It was in Amsterdam that Pearce earned a treasured spot in Australian folklore. In the single sculls, rowed on the city's Sloten Canal, Pearce easily beat opponents from Germany and Denmark to reach the quarter-finals.

There he was matched with a Frenchman by the name of Savrin (no one is quite sure of the gentleman's Christian name). Pearce was doing it easy in the middle of the race, well ahead of his French opponent. Suddenly he heard a loud groan from the crowd. The spectators were pointing furiously at something up ahead. He turned to see what the uproar was all about. There in the middle of the canal was a mother duck and half-a-dozen ducklings swimming in single-file across his path. He stopped to let them pass.

As Pearce waited patiently, the Frenchman caught up and then surged ahead.

Pearce was to later note: 'It's funny now. But it wasn't at the time, for I had to lean on the oars and wait for a clear course. And, all the while, my opponent was pulling away to a five-length lead.'

It mattered not. Pearce was several classes above Savrin and caught him well before the finish line before going away to win by no fewer than 20 lengths. The time of 7 minutes, 42.8 seconds for the 2000-metre row was a new Olympic record, slashing 3.2 seconds off the old mark.

In the semi-final Pearce broke his own world record by 20.2 seconds when beating Theodore Collett of Britain by four lengths and then disposed of the previously unbeaten American Kenneth Myers by four lengths to win the gold medal. Pearce's time of 7 minutes, 11 seconds was a new Olympic record—some 25 seconds better than the previous mark. Incredibly, this record was to stand for more than four decades until Soviet sculler Yuri Malishev took 0.78 of a second off it at the 1972 Munich Olympics.

Contemporary reports say that Pearce wept on the dais when presented with his gold medal, as well as a garland of flowers and a pair of clogs.

The Amsterdam success also won for Pearce the Philadelphia Gold Cup, which went with the Olympic title and represented the Amateur Championship of the World. He was to retain the famous trophy until he eventually turned professional five years later.

What followed Pearce's Olympic success was one of the most disgraceful episodes in world sport. In 1929 he tried to enter the famous Diamond Sculls at the Henley Royal Regatta in England. But snobbery raised its evil head. Pearce was a carpenter by trade—and Henley's rules would not allow any artisans to compete against the gentry. It mattered not to Henley's 'Hooray Henrys' that he was the Olympic champion. It was not the done thing to have members of the lower classes at the hallowed regatta.

Within 12 months Pearce didn't have any job at all. Like so many hundreds of thousands of Australians he had fallen a victim to the ravages of the Great Depression. But he was not forgotten. With the help of friends and rowing authorities he managed to scrape together enough money to go to Canada for the first Empire Games, at Hamilton, in 1930.

It was a foregone conclusion that he should win the gold medal.

'I am pleased to have won,' he said modestly. 'The victory was worth the journey.'

More than he knew at the time!

While he was in Canada, news of Pearce's financial plight reached the ears of whisky magnate Lord Dewar. His Lordship offered him a job in North America as a salesman. This brought an added bonus. The snobs at Henley showed what hypocrites they were, deigning to accept Pearce's entry. After all, he was no longer an artisan, was he? In 1931, he duly won the Diamond Sculls at his first attempt, by six lengths from an Englishman named Bradley, who was competing for Cambridge University's rowing club.

Pearce made it quite clear when accepting the trophy where his heart lay: 'Though I am living in Canada, I am still an Australian.' He followed up that Diamond Sculls success with a second victory a year later.

While still working in Canada, Pearce represented Australia again, at the 1932 Los Angeles Olympics, where he retained his Olympic crown. It was closer this time, with Pearce beating American Bill Miller by half-a-length (just 0.8 seconds between them). But the Australian was never really extended (rating a leisurely 24 strokes to the American's vigorous 40 as they reached the end of the course).

One journalist had the audacity to suggest to Pearce that he had taken it easy to ensure a close finish (and a chance to draw bigger gates when he inevitably turned professional).

The Australian was outraged by the suggestion: 'Sure I took it calmly. There is no other way of rowing a tight race. But you can quote me as saying Bill Miller is the greatest oarsman I have ever met.'

Fate would have it that they would meet again.

In 1933, Pearce turned professional and continued his great success. That same year he met Englishman Ted Phelps for the world professional championship over three miles on Lake Ontario, Canada. A bumper crowd of 30,000 enthusiasts turned up to cheer on the pair. But Phelps was never in the race with the Australian winning easily by 300 yards (275 metres). After the race, Phelps was too exhausted to shake hands, so Pearce just put his arm around his shoulders.

In September the following year, Pearce disposed of a challenge by the 1932 Olympic runner-up, Miller, at Toronto. This time there was no close finish. Pearce won by a massive 15 lengths. One can only surmise at what the journalist who asked the question at the Los Angeles Olympics must have thought.

During 1938, Pearce defended his world crown by beating Australian Evans Paddon (who was eventually to win the title once Pearce had called it a day). The storm clouds of war then intervened and Pearce joined the Canadian navy, where he rose to the rank of Lieutenant Commander.

Once the hostilities were over, he was happy to take on the next generation of scullers. But when none was to be found he retired. At the time a survey of readers by the Australian magazine *Sports Novels* had him in the top 10 Aussie sports stars of all time. Sadly, by the time he died of a heart attack in 1976, most fans were largely ignorant of the exploits of this greatest of all rowers.

Like Father Like Son

Norm O'Neill was one of the most exciting Australian cricketers of the 1950s and '60s. In 42 Tests he scored almost 2800 runs, with six centuries including a high of 181, at the Gabba against the West Indies in the famous Tied Test of 1960.

But his career got away to an inauspicious start. He made his first-class debut, for New South Wales against South Australia, in 1955. He was bowled, with his off-stump uprooted, for 0 off the second ball he received.

In 1979, Norm's son, Mark, made his senior debut, also for New South Wales. In a flukish dismissal, he, too, was bowled off stump off the second ball, for a duck.

The Record Flight of Mark the Magpie

Footballers in various codes come and go. Some *do* stick around longer than others—either on or off the field.

While still running around, Hawthorn's Michael Tuck made 426 senior AFL appearances and half-a-dozen others have topped the 350 mark. Rugby league, on the other hand, has seemed to have taken its toll, with only three making it past 300 first-grade games, with Terry Lamb turning out 349 times for Wests and Canterbury to claim number one spot.

But quite frankly, no one in either code has a record that can compare with that of Mark the Magpie, the long-suffering mascot of Western Suburbs in the NRL. He's not quite certain of the exact figure of his senior appearances, but rest assured it is well over 500. No other mascot comes within a squawk of him. Even South Sydney rugby league's Reggie the Rabbit, who started his stint a season before the Magpie failed to outlast him. And Reggie missed a lot of games when confined to his hutch with illness.

The Magpie, alias Mark Wallington, first donned the feathers in the middle of the 1978 season. And 20 years later he has missed only five matches (including once because he was getting married on the day). He has appeared at almost every first-grade game, all the midweek knockouts (Amco Cup, KB Cup, Panasonic Cup etc) before they were scrapped, games in the now-defunct pre-season Tooheys Challenge and the end-of-year playoff matches. When Wests' minor grades reached the semi-finals he was there, too.

And he's also done his bit for the schoolboys. At the time Wests were based at Lidcombe Oval, near where the stadium for the 2000 Olympics will hold pride of place, their junior area included the inner-western suburb of Ryde. So when Holy Cross, Ryde, won the Commonwealth Bank Cup in 1981 (with future Test player Ben Elias leading the charge) Mark the Magpie donned a Holy Cross jumper and urged them on. And when the Magpies moved to Campbelltown, south-west of the New South Wales capital in 1987, he changed allegiances and helped inspire the local St Gregory's side to victory in several finals (which we reckon is a fair thing, as Mark Wallington was a St Greg's old boy after all).

'People have always thought I'm crazy and they are probably right,' says the 38-year-old Mark, who is the only person other than a player or an official to have been honoured with Wests' life membership (or come to think of it, a similar honour for any other sporting club). 'After all, what grown man spends his spare time leaping around dressed up in feathers, pretending to be a bird?

'It all started off pretty low key, but I soon built up my routine. And I reckon that through all those years, I've provided some pretty good entertainment.'

It all began during a discussion at an after-match barbecue at Lidcombe Oval in 1978. Margaret Raudonikis, the mother of famous Test halfback and later Wests and New South Wales State of Origin coach Tommy, was a big wheel in the Wests Supporters' Club. She asked Mark, who used to help cook the snags and steaks, whether he'd like the job.

At first it was pretty basic stuff. Lead out the team—and then disappear. But soon there was real choreography. Mark would dance with the cheer girls (from both sides) at half-time, do backflips when Wests happened to score a try and collapse, as if dead, when the opposition scored. Needless to say, in recent years, he's spent a lot of time collapsing in a heap.

By day, Mark was a mild-mannered share registration auditor with a giant finance group. Come the weekend and the transformation took place.

'Basically, I've always been pretty shy,' he explained. 'But when I put on the suit I got a bit of Dutch courage. By hiding behind the costume I could do what I really want to do.'

It was not always smooth sailing. In the dim distant past the fires in more than a few romances were doused once the girlfriends found out what he did on the weekends.

'Quite a number gave me the flick,' he recalled. 'They didn't think I was the full quid.'

One didn't give him the brush-off—although she was pretty astounded when he worked up the courage to tell her his deep, dark secret.

He met his wife Pauline through a ballroom dancing group. She wasn't too happy about the Magpie and he considered giving it up once they got married. But when the knot was tied in 1991 ... well, we ask you, what would Wests be without the Magpie?

Mark reckoned the ballroom dancing helped him in his sideline routines.

'It helped shape the character of the Magpie,' he said. 'Especially the Latin-American dancing. All that energy and excitement. It's something I've always taken with me when I've run onto the field.'

He had hoped to channel all that energy into the Sydney Olympics. But the boffins charged with the job of making the 2000 Games a success squashed the hopes of this quiet family man.

It wasn't as if he was looking to join the gravy train ... hoping for a millionaire's salary. He had no desire to become a celebrity himself. He didn't want to rub shoulders with the likes of Olympic chief Juan Antonio Samaranch.

But Mark Wallington *did* want to strut the world stage. Well, not quite strut. More a case of dance. Perhaps a happy wave to millions of people around the world. A friendly gesture to kids and old ladies alike. A somersault or two to show his pride in being a dinki-di Aussie.

Long before the organisers decided on three mascots for Sydney's Olympics, Mark Wallington had offered his services. Sadly, his pleas were lost in a sea of red tape and in-fighting among people jockeying for a slice of the financial action associated with the Games. CVs sent to the SOCOG office in Sydney, phone calls, testimonials from high-profile media personalities and civic and charity leaders were ignored. It was especially disheartening since the Magpie's local MP was the Olympics Minister Michael Knight.

So it looks as if his claim to fame will have to remain with his long unfinished career with Wests.

He's had one black eye and one white eye for as long as he can remember, being an avid collector of Wests' footy cards in the first great collecting craze a quarter of a century ago.

He refused to name the best Wests' player he's seen for fear of offending friends. But names such as John Dorahy, Tom Raudonikis, Les Boyd, John Donnelly and John Ribot, all former Test players, spring to mind. And Bruce 'Bruiser' Clark was one of the most loyal Wests' players he ever saw, reluctantly leaving the club when they were kicked out of the competition in 1983, but pleading with Cronulla to be allowed to return when Wests won their court fight to stay in the race.

The Mapgies are now faced with another fight to stay alive. But Wallington is undeterred.

'Wests have always had a team of honest triers,' said Mark the Magpie. 'Sadly, you need more than that to stay in the big league or to win a Premiership. But I will never give up hope. We're still alive. And, who knows, that elusive big one—the Premiership—may perhaps be just around the corner.'

Hope springs eternal in the heart of the Magpie!

Oldie but Goodie

We're indebted to the old *Turf Monthly* magazine for unearthing what is probably the oldest racehorse ever to win a race. The hayburner named Rocket was no second-rater having won the Perth Cup in 1881 at the mature age of 13. Not a great deal else is known about Rocket except for its last recorded victory, in the Easter Handicap at York some 100 kilometres east of the Western Australian capital. The date was 3 April 1888. And by that time the grand old galloper would have been 20 years of age!

All Arms and Legs

It was no wonder they gave cricketer Alan Thomson the nickname 'Froggy'. The first time spectators saw him bowl they would shake their heads in disbelief. He had a grotesque bowling action. He would bound into the wicket like some hyperactive frog and, with a windmill action and a skip off the wrong foot at the point of delivery, he would send down his fast-medium balls.

The fans loved his boyish enthusiasm and weird style and would cheer his every delivery.

When he was a teenager in Melbourne during the late 1950s, coaches had tried to get him to alter his style to conform to normal cricket thinking. When he tried to do so, he lost all hope of picking up wickets.

Sadly, Froggy Thomson's ability in the first-class cricket arena did not quite match his flamboyant mannerisms, although during his debut season for Victoria (1968–69) it seemed it might. Especially when he snared 5/76 and 6/84 against Gary Sobers' touring West Indians.

The Test selectors finally gave him the nod when the traditional foe, England, toured in 1970–71. After at first being confused by his weird action in the match against Victoria, the Poms knuckled down and showed that Froggy needed more than the surprise element to get Test wickets.

In his Test debut at the Gabba, Thomson managed just 1/136 and 0/20. At the WACA Ground in Perth his figures were 2/118 and 1/71. At the MCG he fared a little better with 3/110 and 0/26. And his one-season Test career came to an end in

Adelaide where he took 2/94 and 3/79, the latter when the Englishmen were going for quick runs to try to force victory.

Froggy Thomson continued in Sheffield Shield for three more seasons, but his unique style of bowling was never again seen internationally. More's the pity!

A Round or Two for a Pound or Two!

The annual show has, for generation after generation, been an integral part of country life. For the cow-cockies it was time to show off their prized sheep, cattle and porkers—and hopefully earn a reputation which would increase the stud fees of their stock. For the ladies of the Country Women's Association (CWA) it was a chance to prove who was the best jam or pickle maker or who could crochet the best doily.

But to most of the folk, especially in the pre-television era, the real attraction was sideshow alley. There they would find 'the lovely Sarita, who will perform the sensual dance of the seven veils' and the bearded lady or the girl in the goldfish bowl. There was the rifle range where they were invited to compete for kewpie dolls ... and, of course, there was the boxing tent.

There were many exponents of these fisticuffs freak shows such as Snowy Flynn and Roy Bell. But the daddy of them all was Jimmy Sharman. He would strut a stage at the front of his tent. Behind him were larger-than-life paintings of some of Australia's boxing legends. Les Darcy, Bill Squires and Tommy Uren and in later years Vic Patrick, Tommy Burns and Jimmy Carruthers. Blokes the country folk had only read about in the sporting pages of the *Herald*. Sharman's boxers would line up alongside him in vividly coloured silk dressing gowns. At one end a boxer would thump on a bass drum and at the other end another would ring a brass bell to gain attention.

Once spectators had gathered in sufficient numbers, Sharman would give a piercing whistle through the microphone. That was the cue for the pair to stop banging the drum and ringing the bell.

'Do I see any likely lads down there among you?' Sharman would shout. 'Who'll take a glove? Who'll take a glove against one of my boys? A round or two for a pound or two.'

And he would be almost knocked over in the rush by the local lads. It was to be a profitable career for the former boxer.

Sharman was well able to handle himself in the ring and only turned to touring when his boxing career was over.

It's hard to dig out the truth about his life because he was a great self-publicist and would regularly change his story to impress the more gullible journalists. But it is believed he was born into a very poor family on a dairy farm at Narellan, south-west of Sydney, on 20 June 1887. Such was the poverty of the Sharmans that none of the 13 children had shoes and allegedly Jimmy's shirts were made out of flour sacks.

He would tell reporters that his grandfather had been a champion bare-knuckle fighter in Ireland—although there are no contemporary reports to either prove or disprove this.

Sharman would explain how he had his first fights at a show at nearby Camden at the age of 11, winning a shilling. But it seems a bit far-fetched that even the exploitative fight promoters of the time would have allowed someone so young into the ring. At 15 he is supposed to have won several bouts in a sideshow at a race meeting at Campbelltown some eight miles (13 kilometres) away and, having won almost 12 quid, decided on a life as a boxer and ran away from home. But it

JIMMY SHARMAN

is more likely that the Campbelltown success actually happened when he was 19 and at that age he was already master of his own destiny. But Sharman was liberal when it came to embellishing the facts.

Over the next few years Sharman had a fight at least once a fortnight around Cowra in the New South Wales central west before moving south to the Riverina, the mecca for so many men lured by the prospect of work on the new Murrumbidgee Irrigation Scheme. The workers needed entertainment and Sharman and other pugs were able to provide it.

Sharman, a natural lightweight, built up a formidable record said to have been 83 knockout wins in 84 bouts. The other fight ended controversially. It was one of two memorable bouts against Sydney boxer Jack Carter at the Olympic Skating Rink in Wagga Wagga.

The fight took place on Friday, 23 August 1912, the night of the Wagga Show. The bout was scheduled for 20 rounds with a winner-take-all purse of £109 and a £20 side bet. The fight finished in the sixth round after Carter slipped through the ropes and injured a leg when landing on the floor. When he was unable to stand up the referee told Sharman that unless he would agree to share the purse with Carter he (the referee) would refuse to give his decision as to who had won the bout. When Sharman would not agree, the bout was declared a no contest and the purse withheld.

The pair met again a couple of months later with Sharman giving Carter a terrible beating, breaking his jaw, before the referee stopped the fight in the nineteenth round. The unconscious Carter was taken to hospital, where he remained for 19 weeks suffering severe medical complications. A newspaper report noted: 'His [Carter's] chances of recovery are causing grave anxiety amongst his relatives and well-wishers. No one feels the position at the present time more keenly than Sharman, who appealed in the contest several times for the towel to be thrown in, as he knew he had the mastery of his opponent.'

There are so many differing stories concerning this fight. One suggests Sharman donated his winnings to the Temora Hospital. Another is that Sharman, so traumatised by the realisation of how badly he had injured Carter, decided there and then to retire.

There are other stories that his retirement only came about after a bottle of ammonia exploded and damaged his eyes. But it is now believed that this incident happened well after he had quit the ring and turned to promoting.

He did make a comeback for one fight in 1920 against a fighter named Jack Smith. It was staged in Temora and Sharman won in three rounds. Maybe this was the actual fight in which Sharman donated his winnings to the hospital—£60. At the very least, he was given honorary membership of the hospital soon after.

In the early days Sharman's boxing troupe travelled by train, but later as country roads became better he'd have his own truck and cars to transport his tents and entourage.

He was the ultimate showman. He understood the racial prejudices of many of those who came to watch. One of his lifetime friends and business partners was Chinese boxer Rud Kee, who fought off scores of challenges from country bigots who reckoned Chinese were inferior to Anglo-Saxons ... and found to their dismay that they certainly weren't. Others would pay their money in the hope that Sharman's Aboriginal boxers would get beaten by white fighters.

Lots of former champions, their big pay-days well and truly over, would finish their careers in Sharman's tent. And it is authenticated that in the early days of his troupe former greats Darcy and Squires were seconded as referees.

Jimmy Sharman retired in 1958, handing over to his son Jimmy Jnr, a former fine rugby league fullback with Western

Suburbs in the Sydney Premiership competition. He in turn shut up shop 13 years later. The death-knell was sounded by strict, new legislation in New South Wales. It demanded that before any fight, both boxers be given a strict medical examination. No one could fight more than one bout in a week. And if knocked out a fighter must have a month's rest. As tent fighters often fought four and five times in a day, they could not adhere to the laws.

The curtain was finally rung down at the Shepparton Show in October 1971. Jimmy Snr had passed away six years earlier on 18 November 1965, at Camden Hospital just up the road from where he had been born.

But the Sharman name remained at Sydney's Royal Easter Show for another quarter of a century. On the same spot where boxers bashed the living daylights out of each other, it was left to dodgem cars to provide the slam-bam action. Needless to say, it was nowhere near as colourful.

Newk Falling in Love Again

You'd have to be the keenest of tennis buffs to know the name of Allan Kendall. He was playing in the golden age of Australian tennis in the 1950s, when the spotlight was on such luminaries as Frank Sedgman, Lew Hoad, Ken McGregor and John Newcombe.

But he was a useful player, with enough ability to survive on the world circuit, which in those days was allegedly amateur ... just like rugby union was until a couple of years ago when the players got by quite nicely, thank you very much. Brown paper bags abounded.

Kendall also dabbled in writing, publishing a book, *Australia's Wimbledon Champions*, about the 11 Aussie men and two women who have won the unofficial world championship.

If you happen to read the small print on the cover of the book you'll find out that Allan Kendall was much more than a tennis player and, through his day job, profoundly influenced a couple of generations of Australian children.

For it was Kendall who was at the helm back in 1966 when the ABC decided to start a new children's television show, 'Play School'. And he guided it through its first 20 years of production.

'I was a most unlikely choice for "Play School",' says Kendall. 'I knew nothing about children. Absolutely nothing at all. I had been one once upon a time. But that is as far as it went.'

What Kendall did have was experience in amateur stage production and a zest for living. The boffins at the ABC reckoned that was enough. Suffice to say, 'Play School' is still going strong more than three decades later.

Kendall has always been proud of the way 'Play School' came to be respected in the acting profession. Thanks to 'Play School' many of the big names of Australian stage and screen got their start in the industry. Names such as John Waters, Lorraine Bayly and Noni Hazlehurst.

'Most actors say it is the most difficult thing they have done,' Kendall explains. 'It takes a rare, rare talent to succeed on "Play School". You see, actors don't have a role to hide behind. I call it naked work.'

You may be wondering what all this has got to do with sport. Well, it's a lead-in to the story of one of sport's most bizarre annual events, where some of the greatest tennis players in history took part in what one may call a French farce. A stage freak show.

And Kendall was the mastermind.

It took place in a most unlikely location—Monte Carlo, on the French Riveria.

During Kendall's tennis days, the capital of Monaco hosted a big annual tournament. Each year, after it was over, one of the local society ladies, millionairess Gloria Butler, would throw a lavish dinner at the Monte Carlo Casino.

And traditionally the tennis players, winners and losers alike, would take part in a theatrical floor show. It was Kendall's job to produce the revue, with the casino providing the orchestra and all the lavish costumes.

'All the big names of tennis took part,' he recalled. 'They would rehearse every night after the day's on-court action.'

According to Kendall, the two best performers were three-times Wimbledon champion John Newcombe and his Aussie Davis Cup teammate Fred Stolle. One year Newk did a Marlene Dietrich impersonation, seductively dressed in black lace, fish-net stockings and wearing stilettos. Newk sang one of Dietrich's most famous hits, 'Falling in Love Again'. He brought the house down.

Stolle was almost as good as Shirley Temple, miming and tap dancing 'On the Good Ship Lollipop'. The BBC immortalised the performances in a special TV documentary.

'No one remembers who won the tournament that year, but everyone remembers who played Marlene and Shirley,' Kendall would explain with pride.

Kendall started producing the revues in 1958, before his 'Play School' days. Once the children's TV show got under way, Kendall would make sure he took a vacation around the time of the tournament. Like many of the tennis players who came back after they had quit the circuit, Kendall wouldn't miss the revues for anything or anyone.

They continued until 1972 when the introduction of open tennis and the huge costs of running a tournament forced an end to the Monte Carlo tournament.

On the sporting front, Kendall continued playing wherever possible on the senior circuit.

'I was born at the right time,' Kendall said. 'In my day tennis was a sport played by sportsmen. It's not like that today. I was privileged to have played against eight of the 11 Australian men who won Wimbledon (including his uncle, Jack Crawford, who won in 1933). I doubt whether more than a couple of others could make that claim.'

And don't bother asking him who was the best. He's too much of a gentleman to give an opinion.

But we *can* report he speaks highly ... very highly ... of Uncle Jack!

A Living Doll

There are not too many sporting champions who can go out in a blaze of glory. Retiring while ruling the roost. Back in 1997, the owners of champion greyhound Tenthill Doll understood this only too well. It was around Easter time and they shed more than a few tears for the dog they knew as 'Sally' as she was forced to call it a day.

Of course, they never admitted their distress. Greyhound racing is a sport for working-class people. And working-class people may cry, but only in the confines of their own home—out of the sight of friends and acquaintances.

Sally's owners knew exactly how Don Bradman must have felt that fateful August day in 1948 at The Oval in London. He needed just four runs to retire from Test cricket with an average of 100. But Eric Hollies wandered in from the direction of the Houses of Parliament, threw over his arm and bowled 'The Don' second ball for a duck in his last Test innings.

Did Bradman have a tear in his eye that day after Hollies and his English teammates had given him three rousing cheers?

Or what about boxer Jimmy Carruthers, Australia's first universally recognised world champion who retired unbeaten after 19 fights? He decided upon a fateful comeback seven years later and made a fool of himself, losing his last bout on a foul to a nobody on the international scene called Jimmy Cassidy.

Then there was the great rugby league player Graeme Langlands, who bumbled his way through the 1975 grand final, the victim of a pain-killing injection in his leg, as his beloved St George got hammered 38–nil. His embarrassment was exacerbated by the fact that he wore white boots and stood out like the legendary lighthouse at Alexandria.

Langlands tried to expunge that memory with a couple of games the following season but when he couldn't produce the goods he retired.

And, of course, there was the gallant racehorse Dulcify, who had to be destroyed after breaking down in the 1979 Melbourne Cup.

So it was with Tenthill Doll. In her last race she finished an ignominious last in the final of the world's richest dog race, the Eukanuba Golden Easter Egg at Sydney's Wentworth Park. She tore a hip-support muscle and would never race again. And when historians look at details of her record the fact that she finished stone motherless last in her final appearance will be there in cold hard print. Or perhaps, in this age of surfing the Net, in vivid colour on the computer screen.

Last of eight at Wentworth Park.

What the computer screen will not show is the emotion behind that and all of Tenthill Doll's 56 starts, 31 of which she won and only eight which she did not make it into a place.

It will not show how the battlers—those residents of the so-called 'Struggle Street' of society—used to flock to dog tracks around Australia to watch this brilliant black bitch regularly dish-lick the opposition. And when she didn't win they still cheered her courageous efforts in trying to get there first.

On the web-sites there will be explanations of how, when her owners called it a day, she had won more prizemoney than any other greyhound that ever raced in Australia—$383,660. And they will show she was the only dog to have won the biggest three races in the nation (the Golden Easter Egg, the Perth Cup and the Australian Cup in Melbourne)—and win them in succession, breaking track records as she qualified for the respective finals.

But how can you show love and affection on the Internet? Pictures, facts and figures can't convey what ordinary Australians felt about Sally.

'I sometimes watch the video of her biggest win, the 1996 Golden Easter Egg, when she came from behind to take the race against all odds,' said part-owner Ray Richards, himself a sporting champion (in 1974, one of the only Australian team in history to reach the finals of soccer's World Cup).

'The grandstand erupted as she reached the front. The fans leaped so high in the air that you can't see the finish of the race on the video because there are so many arms waving around in front of the camera.

'We had hoped she would have won the Egg a second time and gone on to win the other two big races as well. But we were probably only kidding ourselves. It's just that we would have liked her to go out on top.'

According to Richards, they were kidding themselves because Sally had only just recovered from a major operation to insert pins in her two front paws.

She'd been out of action for seven and a half months. The operations had also cost her the chance to win the (greyhound)

Melbourne Cup which could have netted her a $100,000 first-prize plus a bonus of $100,000 for the Australian–Melbourne Cups double.

Richards and a mate Matthew Valenti bought the bitch in May 1995 after she had 13 starts for six wins and five placings in Queensland. She was named after her home town of Tent Hill, south-east of Toowoomba.

That's also where she got her kennel name of Sally.

'It suited her,' said Richards. 'I never knew anyone called Sally. But I envisage if I did, they'd have been nice, spirited ladies. Just like our little Sally.

'She cost us $20,000. We bought her on the advice of Harry Sarkis who trained her with Carol Giniotis. Good advice? You bet it was!

'I remember being on a high after making the World Cup finals in Germany a quarter of a century ago. But nothing can compare with having a champion like Tenthill Doll.

'It sounds silly, but she was like a four-legged daughter. And all the fans around the country reacted like she was their cousin.

'We'd have liked her to have gone out a winner. History will show she didn't. But that won't in any way dim the love the fans had for her. She was ... and will continue to be ... Super Sally!'

The 'Modest' Professor Miller

There was certainly no doubting the incredible ego of William Miller. A century later we shook our heads at the effrontery of Cassius Clay (later Muhammad Ali) when he told us all 'I am the greatest'. The fact that he proved to be just that was beside the point. It was that he dared to point out the obvious that had us shaking our heads with amazement.

But Miller had perfected the art of self-aggrandisement so well that even Ali would have acknowledged the perfection he had achieved. Miller had no university degree but called himself 'Professor'. Professor of what? To this day, no one really knows. And he happily advertised himself as the 'Champion Athlete of the World', despite never having won any title recognised outside his coterie of backslappers in Australia.

To be fair, the good professor was an exceptionally fine all-round sportsman. He toured the United States during the 1870s taking on anyone who would dare to challenge him in boxing, wrestling, athletics, fencing and the lifting of dumb-bells. And, we suspect, in a few other sports as well, although there are no records of this. 'Can you beat the Australian Strongman?' the posters would ask—ignoring the fact that Miller was born in Britain. Reference to the fact that he was from the wild colony Down Under, where men were men and women just looked on in admiration, brought in more spectators than any suggestion that he was from across the Atlantic.

THE 'MODEST' PROFESSOR MILLER 159

PROFESSOR WILLIAM MILLER
A contemporary artist's impression of the professor's 1884 bout with Scottish champion Donald Dinnie. (Miller is wearing the black shorts.)

Back home in Sydney the professor cashed in on the publicity he had generated in America. There were references in the local press that on Monday, 17 October 1881, he put on a charity show at the Sydney School of Arts. He was said to have been assisted by his colleague, Professor D'Harcourt and a dozen students from their gymnasium at Liverpool, west of the city. Again one must wonder about the academic qualifications of his mate. At the very least the team put on a splendid performance of 'athletic skills' and artistic poses that represented statues of sports men and women in various poses. There were also, we are told, tricks on the horizontal and parallel bars.

Miller was the star, performing a couple of his favourite tricks. He used his right arm, keeping it straight, to lift above his head a 180 pound (82 kilogram) dumb-bell. Then, using his left arm, in the same manner he lifted a 60 pound (27 kilogram) dumb-bell over his head six or seven times.

At one time Miller was the centre of a storm when he refereed an Australian boxing championship bout at the Richmond Crystal Palace in Melbourne. He refused to give his casting vote when the two judges disagreed on the victor—Peter Jackson, the West Indian-born reigning champion, or the pride of Broken Hill, Joe Goddard. The professor declared it a draw and the fans almost tore down the building.

Miller's ego also got the better of him one day when being interviewed in the Melbourne Athletic Club by a sporting journalist. The writer hit a raw nerve when he noted that a Frenchman named Francois had set a world record for dumbbell lifting in London. Miller frowned at the journalist and, with not a word, took off his jacket, put his feet together and calmly lifted two 56 pound (25 kilogram) dumb-bells, one in each hand, over his head 20 times—twice the number of lifts performed by Francois.

'I told you I am the Champion Athlete of the World,' Miller sniffed before putting his jacket back on.

CHEERS!

CLARENCE WHISTLER

The good professor may have had a big ego. But he did have a big reputation, too. Some of the finest wrestlers in the world came to Australia to challenge for his 'World Championship'. Libnan Ayoub, the son of a 1970s grappler Sheik Wadi Ayoub, has researched the sport for a book he published on '100 Years of Australian Professional Wrestling'. And he reports the most unfortunate finale to a Professor William Miller bout.

An intriguingly named American, Clarence Whistler, had won a World Tournament in St Louis and journeyed Down Under to prove that it was he, not Miller, who was the best. They faced each other in the ring at Melbourne's Theatre Royal on 26 September 1885. After a gruelling bout that lasted two hours, Whistler emerged successful. He *was* the undisputed World Champion.

At that moment he should have called it a day ... or, as the case may be ... a night.

But, no! Clarence wanted to celebrate in a manner that had made him famous. He toasted his success with a glass of champagne. According to contemporary reports, he then chewed up the empty glass and swallowed it. His entourage cheered. After all, it was Clarence's usual party trick. It had always worked in the past.

Sadly, this time a sliver of glass pierced his gullet and he died in agony a few hours later. He never made it back to the United States—being buried in a long-lost grave in a Melbourne cemetery.

But perhaps Miller's greatest claim to fame is his well-documented bout with the great boxer Larry Foley. It was conducted under the Marquess of Queensberry rules at the Academy of Music in Castlereagh Street, Sydney, on 28 May 1883. The unbeaten Foley had been lured out of retirement for the contest. He was out of condition, but the purse was too good to ignore. The two scrappers fought it out for more than three hours. Miller was clearly the better, raining blow after blow on the luckless Foley. Eventually the hundreds of punches began to tell. In the thirty-seventh round and again in the fortieth, Foley slumped to the ground. On the latter occasion he couldn't get back to his feet. But a second dragged him from the ring. The professor claimed victory, but the referee shook his head.

The pair readied themselves for the forty-first round. It was then that a couple of Foley's cronies leaped into the ring between the combatants and began punching each other. Police in the crowd intervened and called off the fight . . . much to the delight of the Foley supporters who had bet vast sums on their man retaining his unbeaten record.

Miller may not have officially won the fight. But saner minds prevailed and he was awarded the £500 winner's purse. The 'Champion Athlete of the World' had again prevailed!

Topping the Averages

There was no denying the bowling ability of Victorian cricketer Bill Johnston. Had he not been around at the same time as that great fast bowling duo of Ray Lindwall and Keith Miller he would have got more opportunities with the new ball and he may very well have been up there with the greats of the game.

His 160 wickets in 40 Tests are a good indication of his worth. Oh, yes, if required he could bowl a bit of spin, too. It's a cliché, but as a batsman Johnston made a good bowler. In a decade of first-class cricket he arrived at the crease 162 times,

BILL JOHNSTON
As a batsman he made a good bowler

almost always batting number 11. His highest score was just 38 runs.

For all this, Johnston holds a place in the annals of cricket history for his batting performances on the 1953 tour of England. The Australian team included some fellows who could wield the willow with dramatic effect. Blokes like Miller and Alan Davidson (two of the greatest all-rounders the world of cricket has known), Neil Harvey (with a Test best of 205), Lindsay Hassett (whose 16,890 runs in first-class cricket was at the time second only among Australians to the legendary Don Bradman) and Arthur Morris (whose highest first-class score was 290).

Yet when the tour was over who led the batting averages? None other than the confirmed rabbit, Bill Johnston! His average was 102, earned through a quirk of statistics. Johnston batted 17 times on tour, but was dismissed only once. Hence, all his tiny scores added together put him ahead of the top-flight batsmen.

Johnston laughed about it all: 'It was the result of a combination of application, concentration and dedication. And as the adage says—class always tells.'

But Johnston did have a bit of help late in the tour. In the final couple of matches—social or so-called festival games—Hassett was known to offer some friendly advice to the opposition bowlers on the importance of Johnston remaining not out, thus ensuring his coveted average. And, after all, dismissing a rabbit held little kudos. Being part of history was an entirely different matter.

D-Day for Normanby

Racing historians will delight in telling you that the world's youngest jockey was the famous Australian-born Frank Wootton, who was legged up for the first time in Johannesburg, South Africa, in 1903, when he was just nine years and 10 months old. The fact that young Wootton went on to become one of the greatest jockeys in the world has a lot to do with the story.

But talk to folks out in the west of New South Wales and they will swear blue blind that Joseph Burton was younger. Not that they can prove it, mind you. But local folklore suggests that he started riding around the age of eight. Maybe even earlier! It was just that his first big win, at Orange in 1862, came when he was 10. It was on a horse called Vixen. Just ask any local and he or she will tell you.

They'll also explain that young Joe weighed just 3 stone, 10 pounds, wringing wet. That's 23.6 kilograms in today's measurements. Oh, yes. And he stood only 4 feet, 7 inches (140 centimetres) tall.

Is it any wonder they dubbed young Joe 'Tom Thumb'?

Tom ... um ... Joe never really made it as a jockey. Sure, he rode a few winners around the west. But along the way someone suggested that he might make a better trainer than a jockey.

To cut a long story short (and the pun is intentional), he did!

In the mid-1880s he was given a horse called Normanby to train. As far as nags go, Normanby showed plenty of promise. But he had problems with his hooves. Near a cripple he was. Normanby went from one trainer to another. Down the line, so to speak, until he got to Tom Thumb. Each and every trainer laughed at the thought that Burton would even bother to try with the wretch of a horse.

Was it love, or just perseverance, that triumphed?

Tom Thumb Burton saddled up Normanby for the Sydney Gold Cup of 1885. He was ridden by a lightweight jockey called Nicholson, who had to add lead to the saddle-bags to make the required handicap of 6 stone, 10 pounds (43 kilograms). Just think what dead weight he would have carried if his pint-sized trainer had been in the saddle.

Suffice to say that the said Normanby won the Sydney Cup. Tom Thumb Burton invited all the previous trainers of the said hayburner for a drink at the bar.

Funny enough, not one turned up. As King Solomon was wont to say: 'Jealousy is cruel as the grave!'

The Greatest of Them All?

The disabled will tell you how the attitudes of able-bodied members of the community have changed in recent years. Remember the days of patronising discomfort? Well, there is now a muted feeling of respect and understanding of some of the problems of the disabled.

But we've still got a helluva way to go. The media coverage of Louise Sauvage shows just how far.

When Kieren Perkins won gold at the Atlanta Olympics

there were pages and pages of hyped newspaper copy and replay after replay on the television news and sports shows. Kieren was the flavour of the moment.

Not so with Louise Sauvage. She managed, at best, a half-page when she won the 800m athletics demonstration event at the Olympics. And when she won four golds at the Paralympics there was even less coverage. You were lucky to catch the briefest of a glimpse of her on TV. She won four gold medals, for heaven's sake!

So it was at the 1997 World Athletics Championship in Athens. There would not have been a person in Australia who missed Cathy Freeman's triumph. And jolly good luck to her, too. Louise Sauvage's gold medal performance rated just a few lines.

But, strange as it may seem, it's never really bothered Sauvage, arguably the most dominant sportswoman Australia has ever produced. Fanny Durack, Betty Cuthbert, Dawn Fraser, Shane Gould ... they were world class. But not in the way Sauvage has been. A freak? Yep, up there with Heather McKay, Walter Lindrum and Don Bradman.

'People are slowly becoming more aware of our successes,' she said. 'By the 2000 Olympics and Paralympics the disabled should be getting some of the recognition they deserve. There is still a long education process. Able-bodied people don't really understand what it is like to have disabilities.

'But seeing us in action is all part of the learning process. Indeed, we are finding people enjoy watching our sport because it is so different.'

It's a well-worn cliché—but her success is a triumph of will over adversity.

She was born with a medical condition known as myleodisplasia, which affects the base of her spinal cord, rendering her legs useless. If that was not enough, Sauvage suffered from scoliosis or lateral curvature of the spine. When she was 13 doctors had to perform an horrendous operation to help correct it, screwing metal rods into the spine, one from in front, the other through her back. It helped a bit, but the spine still has a list of around 45 degrees.

It was after that operation and two years of rehabilitation that she began to really concentrate on athletics. Within a year she was, in 1990, selected to compete in the World Disabled Championships in Holland. It was there that the experts first sat up and took notice of this young athlete from Perth.

Sauvage won the 100 metres in world record time. She then took out gold in the 200 metres. Well, she almost did. She was first across the line and was so delighted she immediately rang her parents, back in Australia. A short while later she had to make a second phone call. She was distraught. Officials had disqualified her for straying from her lane.

'I was devastated at the time,' she recalled. 'But it was a good lesson. I never made that mistake again.'

By the Barcelona Paralympics in 1992 there was hardly anyone in the world who could match her on the track. She won gold in the 100m, 200m and 400m and silver in the 800m. It was the last time she was to be beaten over 800 metres— her favourite distance, even though most of her efforts were later concentrated on the longer road races.

She will never forget the presentation of her first gold medal at Barcelona: 'It was the most memorable moment of my life. I'm not sure if anything will ever top that feeling, with the Australian flag being raised and the national anthem being played. It was a real buzz.'

The year after her Barcelona triumphs she won the first 800m demonstration event at the World Athletics Championships (able-bodied) in the German city of Stuttgart. She won by an incredible seven seconds. That same year she took out road races in the United States, New Zealand and Holland as well as several in Australia.

In 1994, the year she was honoured as the first Australian Paralympian of the Year, she won the 800m, 1500m, 5000m and marathon in the World Disabled Championships. There was a repeat success in the 800m at the 1995 able-bodied titles in Gothenburg, Sweden.

And, of course, another golden year in 1996. The Olympic gold and Paralympic golds in the 400m, 800m, 1500m and 5000m. The 400m success (by almost two seconds) came only an hour after she had won the gruelling 5000m event in world record time. Asked how she managed to summon the energy for her back-up performance, Sauvage laughed: 'I might have been possessed or something.'

After that Herculean effort it was no surprise that she was named Paralympian of the Year for a second time.

In 1997, Sauvage won the one important race that had eluded her for so long. She took out the Boston Marathon at her fifth attempt in what she described as 'the hardest race on the international circuit'. For so long this prestige event had been property of American Jean Driscoll, who had won it seven straight times.

From the start, Sauvage and Driscoll went for it, hammer and tongs, breaking away from the field after just four kilometres of the 42km event. Five kilometres from the finish Sauvage seemed to be getting on top and edged ahead. Then disaster struck Driscoll. One of her wheels got caught in tram tracks and she overturned. Sauvage raced away for an easy win.

'It was less fulfilling, the way I won,' she said. 'It was almost not fair. I felt really bad for her. But I was in front at the time and feeling good after almost losing it earlier in the race, on the hills. Let's hope next time there can be no hiccups and I can beat her again.'

And she did. In the 1998 Boston Marathon there were no hiccups and Sauvage was first across the line again.

Then came her greatest triumph. It was at the 1998 World Paralympic Athletics Championship in the English city of Birmingham. The authorities made it hard for her. They ruled that competitors could only compete in four individual events. It was shades of the 1948 Olympics where the great Dutch athlete Fanny Blankers-Koen wasn't allowed to compete in the long jump and high jump (even though she held the world record in both) because she was also entered in three track races (which she duly won).

But Sauvage still cleaned up in Birmingham. Six golds all told—in the 800m, 1500m and 5000m plus the 4×100m and 4×400m relays. She rated the 4×100m relay win as the most satisfying of her career—because she was part of a team.

Nevertheless, she has always been particularly pleased with her ability to win individual events over all distances.

'It's not as if you see Carl Lewis or Cathy Freeman running in a marathon,' she would say with a deep chuckle.

Touché!

Into the Record Books

Boxer Charlie Hansen has never been keen to discuss what happened on 26 June 1991. And one can't blame him. The editors of the *Guinness Book of Records* are a bit reluctant to accept his record effort, too. But no one invited them along to the Homestead Hotel in Brisbane that night.

What took place that night was the quickest defeat in boxing history—not just in Australia, but anywhere in the world. The 30-year-old Brisbane boxer Arne 'Charlie' Hansen fought his way into the record books. Well, fought is hardly the right word. For hardly a blow was thrown in anger. In a bout at the Homestead Hotel, Hansen's fight with Paul Rees was stopped just five seconds after it started. Yep, five seconds! No more, no less.

After the opening bell sounded, the pair moved into centre-ring. Hansen threw a left-right combination and then let out a yell. 'I can't see, I can't see,' he screamed. And referee Allan Simpson had no alternative but to stop the fight and crown Rees the winner.

Apparently, the inside of Rees' glove had caused a laceration to Hansen's right eye. A fluke injury? His trainer Jim Young noted after the bout: 'Charlie reckoned he'd never make it into the records books for anything. It's probably not an enviable record, but it's a record all the same.'

Sure is!

A Trip Down Memory Lane

There are some things that are indelibly etched on one's mind. Just because you happened to be lucky enough to be there on the right day, at the right time. Flukes? You betcha!

I crave indulgence to tell you about a few personal sporting flukes. The flukes of having been there to witness history. The Melbourne Olympics, Betty Cuthbert, Warner Batchelor and Chilla. Bob Massie at Lord's, a lot of wickets and a West Indian fan who carefully sipped at his Guinness and not only understood my delight but shared it. And a Pom who missed a goal from in front at Wembley—to be remembered forever as the man who lost the biggest match of his career.

FIRST, the Olympics. And I dip my lid to Sir Frank Packer. He was only Mr Packer in those days. But he had decided to look after the kids of Australia and take 50 of us to see the Melbourne Olympics. It was through a series of contests in the magazine called ... blush, blush ... *Chucklers' Weekly*. Those who now laugh can but contemplate what we saw in Melbourne and they never did.

I was 12 years old and took my first tentative steps on what was to eventually be a career in journalism by writing a 50-word piece on 'Why I Like Milk!'. And any War Baby or Baby Boomer who had to stomach the vile, curdled muck that was forced down our throats after it had sat in the Aussie sun in the school playgrounds for several hours would understand how I lied!

It was the greatest lie of my life. But I got my trip to Melbourne.

And we, the lucky few, were all entranced. Betty Cuthbert was indeed the Golden Girl (interviews I have conducted in recent years as she has fought the ravages of MS have only reinforced my opinion). Chilla Porter nearly won the high jump—but we had to leave the Melbourne Cricket Ground early to return to our hotel in the Dandenongs before he finished his sensational duel with American Charlie Dumas.

We didn't get to meet the Americans, including coach and athletics legend Jesse Owens and dual sprint gold medallist Bobby Morrow. Security men had sealed off the Olympic Village on account of the fact that a Greek-born consort to the British monarch was visiting and 50 Aussie kids may have been a security risk. Thanks a bunch, Phil!

Warner Batchelor? Well, he was a flyweight boxer not much bigger than I was and I watched him fight someone— I know not who—and win. Batchelor gave me his autograph and made me a fan for life. Where are you now, Warner?

By the way, our hotel burned down on the second last day we were there. So Warner and Betty and Dawn ... my autograph book with your scribbles went up in flames with all the others. But we didn't care. We had seen history.

(Just a thought! Kerry. Jamie. Any chance of you doing what your dad and granddad did for the kids of today?)

THEN there was Lord's in 1972. A visit to the holy shrine of cricket! I plead guilty to being a typical Australian Norm in wandering with a mate down St John's Wood Road carrying an Esky full of ... I hate to say it ... Reschs. (I'm a VB man now.) A bowler-hatted gent walking the other way looked down his nose and sniffed: 'You're not on the Sydney Cricket Ground Hill now, you know!'

Indeed we weren't. I will not mention the name of the other miscreant, except to say he is today one of Australia's foremost sporting journalists.

We settled down in the stand at the Nursery End. Folk who have listened to the likes of John Arlott and Alan McGilvray will conjure up visions of where we were placed to watch the proceedings.

Next to us was a distinguished West Indian gentleman with a brown paper bag from which he occasionally withdrew long-necked bottles of Guinness. He, too, will remember this day as Bob Massie ripped through the English cricket team. Thanks to the medicine provided by the good Dr Resch, I'm not quite sure exactly which day this was—suffice to say I was ensconced at the Nursery End for the entire Test. Massie skittled the Poms left, right and centre.

And with each wicket the West Indian gent would nod at us and say: 'Isn't it good to see the blighters getting blitzed.' Except he didn't exactly say blighters and he certainly didn't say blitzed. But as my elderly mum will be reading this, those words will suffice.

Seventeen wickets for the match.

Gee, it certainly made up for the previous time I had sat in the very same seats (in 1968) and watched as the Australian cricketers, some who had come straight to the ground from the wedding reception of an Aussie journalist, get routed for 78. Dougie Walters top-scored that day with 26. But he could often score centuries after a night of research, checking whether XXXX was better than Tooheys.

FINALLY there is the story of Don Fox. The saddest sight of my sporting life. A fluke that I was even at Wembley Stadium that Saturday in May 1968. Peed down all morning, it did. There was water up to the players' ankles.

But it would have taken a tidal wave for the officials to have called off the Wembley Rugby League Challenge Cup final.

To cut a long story short, with a minute or so to go, Wakefield Trinity scored a try that put them one point behind Leeds. Fox lined up the simplest of kicks that would win the match. At that moment, some galoot got on the blower and announced to all 100,000 of us, including the bloke that was about to take the kick, that a certain Don Fox had been named Man of the Match.

The simple kick slewed off his boot and the Man of the Match lost the match. That is his legacy. And I was there to see it. Two decades later and I'm still shaking my head in disbelief.

Such is sport!